Reading
Skills

Grade 4

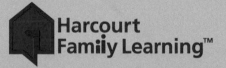

**Harcourt
Family Learning™**

Copyright © 2004 by Spark Educational Publishing
Adapted from *Comprehension Skills Complete Classroom Library*
by Linda Ward Beech, Tara McCarthy, and Donna Townsend
Copyright © 2001 by Harcourt Achieve
Licensed under special arrangement with Harcourt Achieve.

Illustrator: Judy Stead

ISBN 1-4114-0116-6

Please submit changes or report errors to *www.sparknotes.com/errors*
For more information, please visit *www.flashkidsbooks.com*

Printed and bound in China

Spark Educational Publishing
A Division of Barnes & Noble Publishing
120 Fifth Avenue
New York, NY 10011

Dear Parent,

The ability to read well is an important part of your child's development. This book is designed to help your child become a better reader. The wide range of high-interest stories will hold your child's attention and help develop his or her proficiency in reading. Each of the six units focuses on a different reading comprehension skill: finding facts, detecting a sequence, learning new vocabulary through context, identifying the main idea, drawing conclusions, and making inferences. Mastering these skills will ensure that your child has the necessary tools needed for a lifetime love of reading.

Unit 1 contains activities to fine-tune your child's ability to spot facts in a story—a necessary skill for understanding a reading selection. This unit is filled with stories to test your child's understanding of how to identify facts in a story. The focus is on specific details that tell who, what, when, where, and how.

Reading for sequence means identifying the order of events in a story or the steps in a process, and understanding the relationship of one event or step to other events or steps. Unit 2 contains stories that will test your child's understanding of the order of events in a story.

Unit 3 teaches your child how to use context to learn new words. When practicing using context, your child must use all the words in a reading selection to understand the unfamiliar words. This important skill helps a reader understand words and concepts by learning how language is used to express meaning. Mastering this skill ensures that your child will become a successful independent reader.

One of the keys to learning to read well is being able to differentiate between the main point of a reading selection and the supporting details. Unit 4 will help your child learn to recognize the main idea of a story.

Drawing a conclusion is a complex reading skill because a conclusion is not stated in a reading selection. Your child must learn to put together the details from the information as if they were clues to a puzzle. The conclusion must be supported by the details in the reading selection. Unit 5 contains stories to help your child learn to draw conclusions about the passages in the book.

To make an inference, your child must consider all the facts in a reading selection. Then he or she must put together those facts and what is already known to make a reasonable inference about something that is not stated in the selection. Making an inference requires the reader to go beyond the information in the text. Unit 6 will help your child learn how to make inferences.

To help your child get the most from this workbook, encourage your child to read each reading selection slowly and carefully. Explain the purpose of each unit to your child so that he or she has a better understanding of how it will help his or her reading skills. There's an answer key at the end of this workbook. Your child can check the answer key to see which questions he or she got right and wrong. Go back to the questions your child answered incorrectly and go over them again to see why he or she picked the incorrect answer. Completing the activities in this workbook will get your child on the right track to becoming an excellent reader. Continue your child's educational development at home with these fun activities:

- Enlist your child's help when writing grocery lists.
- When preparing a meal, have your child read the recipe aloud.
- Provide entertaining reading selections for your child. Have a discussion about what he or she has read.
- Instead of reading a bedtime story to your child, have your child read a bedtime story to you!
- Write down the directions to a project, such as a gardening project or an arts and crafts project, for your child to read.
- Give your child a fun reading passage and ask him or her to draw a picture about it.
- Ask your child to read road signs and billboards that you encounter during car trips.
- Leave cute notes on the refrigerator or your child's pillow.
- Have your child write and mail a letter to a loved one.
- Ask your child to read the directions for a board game, and then play the game together.
- Bring your child to the library or bookstore so that he or she can choose which great book to read next.

Table of Contents

What Are Facts?

Facts are sometimes called details. They are small pieces of information. Facts can appear in true stories, such as those in the newspaper. They can also appear in tales and other stories that people make up.

How to Read for Facts

You can find facts by asking yourself questions. Ask *who*, and your answer will be a fact about a person. Ask *what*, and your answer will be a fact about a thing. Ask *where*, and your answer will be a fact about a place. Ask *when*, and your answer will be a fact about a time. Ask *how many* or *how much*, and your answer will be a fact about a number or an amount.

Try It!

Read this story and look for facts as you read. Ask yourself *what* and *when*.

The *Titanic*

On April 10, 1912, the *Titanic* left England on its first trip. It was the largest and one of the safest ships ever built. Many rich and famous people were on board. They planned to arrive in New York in six days. But on the night of April 14, the ship ran into an iceberg. The iceberg tore a huge hole in the ship's side. The passengers climbed into lifeboats as the ship began to sink, but there were not enough boats for everyone. Only 711 of the 2,207 people on board lived to tell about the shipwreck.

Did you find these facts when you read the paragraph? Write the facts on the lines below.

◆ What happened to the *Titanic*?

Fact:_____

◆ When did the ship run into the iceberg?

Fact:_____

Practice Finding Facts

Below are some practice questions. The first two are already answered. You can do the third one on your own.

___*B*___ **1.** How many people lived to tell about the shipwreck?
  A. 2,207   **c.** 500
  B. 711   **D.** 947

Look at the question and answers again. The words *how many* are asking for a number. There are many numbers in the paragraph, but you are looking for one that tells how many people lived through the disaster. Read the paragraph until you find the words *lived to tell about the shipwreck.* The sentence says that only 711 of the 2,207 people on board lived. So the correct answer is **B**.

___*C*___ **2.** The *Titanic* was sailing to
  A. England   **c.** New York
  B. Paris   **D.** Iceland

Look at the question. It asks for the name of the place the *Titanic* was sailing to. Search the story for the names of places. You should find this sentence: "They planned to arrive in New York in six days." So the correct answer is **C**.

Now it's your turn to practice. Answer the next question by writing the letter of the correct answer on the line.

_____ **3.** When did the *Titanic* leave England?
  A. April 10, 1912   **c.** June 4, 1912
  B. March 1, 1912   **D.** April 14, 1912

Read each story. After each story you will answer questions about the facts in the story. Remember, a fact is something that you know is true.

First Sign of Spring

How do you know that spring is on its way? For many Americans the first sign of spring is baseball. In late winter many big-league teams head south. They go to training camps in warm states such as Florida and Arizona. There they get ready for the opening of baseball season in early April.

Each team has its own camp. The players spend long days training and getting in shape. They run, hit, throw, and catch. They learn to listen to the coaches and to work together as a team. They also play some practice games against other teams. These are called exhibition games.

Spring training camps are full of hope. New players hope to stay on the team. Other players hope to have their best baseball season. Everyone hopes to be part of a winning team.

_____ 1. For many people baseball is a sign of
    A. season   **C.** spring
    B. work   **D.** winter

_____ 2. Players go to training camps in Florida and
    A. Arizona   **C.** April
    B. Arkansas   **D.** Americans

_____ 3. The players run, hit, throw, and
    A. coach   **C.** camp
    B. catch   **D.** kick

_____ 4. Practice games are called
    A. spring training   **C.** spring games
    B. winning records   **D.** exhibition games

_____ 5. Spring training camps are full of
    A. hope   **C.** trees
    B. bats   **D.** fans

What do baseball teams pack when they go south? The list is very long! One team from New York takes 3,600 baseballs, 360 bats, 200 uniforms, and 75 helmets. Baseball teams also take pitching machines. Many teams take trunks full of medicine and bandages.

Each player also packs things for the trip. Some take bicycles, golf clubs, and beach chairs. Others take their own TV sets. Players taking their children may pack toys and games.

Large vans move the teams to their training camps. Many helpers load and unload the equipment and baggage. By April it's time to move again. The baseball season has begun.

_____ **6.** One team takes along thousands of
        A. helmets   **C.** baseballs
        B. uniforms   **D.** machines

_____ **7.** Baseball teams take machines that
        A. catch   **C.** patch
        B. jog   **D.** pitch

_____ **8.** Players sometimes take their own
        A. bikes   **C.** beds
        B. teams   **D.** boats

_____ **9.** The teams move to training camps in big
        A. planes   **C.** vans
        B. cabs   **D.** workers

_____ **10.** Loading and unloading the trucks takes many
        A. days   **C.** machines
        B. weeks   **D.** helpers

Tale of Tails

Many animals have tails. They use their tails for many different purposes. For instance, some animals use their tails as flyswatters. Have you ever seen a cow flicking its tail back and forth? It's getting rid of bugs. Horses use their tails in this way, too.

Some animals hang by their tails. Monkeys often do this. Then they can use all four of their paws for other things, such as eating. Another animal that uses its tail as a "hanger" is the opossum. The opossum also uses its tail to help it climb trees.

Animals that live in the water use their tails to help them swim. A fish moves its tail from side to side. The rest of its body curves in the opposite direction from its tail. Alligators and crocodiles also swing their tails as they swim. Their large tails give them power and speed.

_____ **1.** Animals use their tails for different
      A. periods   **C.** seasons
      B. purposes   **D.** lengths

_____ **2.** An animal that uses its tail as a flyswatter is the
      A. cow   **C.** hog
      B. fish   **D.** bug

_____ **3.** The monkey uses its tail to
      A. swim   **C.** hang
      B. climb   **D.** talk

_____ **4.** A fish moves its tail
      A. up and down   **C.** in a circle
      B. from side to side   **D.** upside down

_____ **5.** Alligators and crocodiles use their tails for
      A. fishing   **C.** power
      B. flying   **D.** curves

The kangaroo has a large, useful tail. It is like a chair. The kangaroo leans on its tail to rest. The tail is also good for leaping and landing. It helps the kangaroo to keep its balance. This is important because an adult kangaroo can leap as far as 15 feet at a time.

A fox has a big, bushy tail. This is a good tail to have on cold nights. The fox can put its tail over its nose and paws while it sleeps. The tail is a blanket that keeps the fox warm.

Some animals don't keep their tails with them at all times. One example is the lizard. If an enemy pulls the lizard's tail in a struggle, the tail breaks off. The lizard leaves its tail and runs to safety. Don't worry! The lizard will soon grow a new tail.

_____ **6.** The kangaroo uses its tail as a place to
    A. eat   **C.** lean
    B. grow   **D.** leave

_____ **7.** A kangaroo's tail is also helpful for
    A. jumping   **C.** walking
    B. swimming   **D.** crying

_____ **8.** The fox uses its bushy tail as a
    A. pillow   **C.** chair
    B. cover   **D.** brush

_____ **9.** A lizard's tail can help the lizard escape from
    A. friends   **C.** enemies
    B. kangaroos   **D.** blankets

_____**10.** The lizard can grow a new
    A. fin   **C.** nose
    B. leg   **D.** tail

Words Around the Nation

Most people in the United States speak English. But they don't all use the same words for the same things. For instance, what do you call a round, flat breakfast food served with maple syrup? Some people call these *flapjacks*. In other places people call them *griddlecakes*. If you live in the hills of Arkansas or Tennessee, you might answer *flitters*. If you live in Mississippi, you might say *battercakes*. Most people in the United States say *pancakes*.

Suppose you are talking about an insect some people call a *dragonfly*. People in Florida wouldn't know what that means. They call this insect a *mosquito hawk*. People in nearby Georgia don't know what a mosquito hawk is. They call the very same insect a *snake doctor*! Still another word for dragonfly is *snake feeder*.

_____ **1.** People describe things using different
    A. works   **C.** plants
    B. words   **D.** sights

_____ **2.** A dragonfly is a kind of
    A. insect   **C.** doctor
    B. pancake   **D.** monster

_____ **3.** Another word that means *flapjack* is
    A. carrot cake   **C.** griddlecake
    B. dragonfly   **D.** slapjack

_____ **4.** A dragonfly is also called a
    A. snake doctor   **C.** snake nurse
    B. snakeroot   **D.** snapdragon

_____ **5** The word *mosquito hawk* is used by people in
    A. Oregon   **C.** Tennessee
    B. Arkansas   **D.** Florida

Do you want to build a fire? Building a fire might not be very easy if you live in the United States. One language expert has found 169 different words for the wood used to start a fire. Some of these words are *lighterd knots*, *kindling wood*, and *lightning wood*.

Let's go shopping. Do you want cling peaches, plum peaches, green peaches, or pickle peaches? It doesn't matter. They are all the same thing. It just depends on where you are.

Once you buy your fruit, you can put it in a paper bag, a sack, or even a poke. You can eat it at home on your porch, veranda, or gallery. You might want to invite your friend or buddy to share the snack, chow, or grub. Don't eat the pits, though. They will make you sick no matter what you call them!

_____ **6.** You use kindling wood to
    A. build a porch   **C.** build a house
    B. start a fire   **D.** plant trees

_____ **7.** A *poke* is a
    A. paper   **C.** sack
    B. plum   **D.** pig

_____ **8.** How many words mean the same as *lighterd knots*?
    A. 196   **C.** 16
    B. 168   **D.** 96

_____ **9.** A green peach is the same as a
    A. cling peach   **C.** red plum
    B. pink peach   **D.** green plum

_____ **10.** Some Americans say *gallery* instead of
    A. porch   **C.** kitchen
    B. pooch   **D.** vessel

Wonder Worker

You have probably heard the saying "busy as a beaver." This saying is really true. Beavers are almost always working.

The beaver is a builder. This furry animal builds dams and tunnels. It builds a home called a lodge. The beaver's tools for this work are a broad, flat tail and strong front teeth.

The first thing a beaver does is build a dam. Beavers build their dams across quiet streams where no other beavers live. They use their powerful teeth to cut down trees. Then they use their teeth to make the trees into logs about 6 feet long. They drag the logs across the stream to the dam. Beavers also use leaves and branches in their dams. They pack them together with mud to make a wall. The beaver's wide tail is handy for slapping the mud into place. When it is finished, the wall of a beaver dam is strong enough to keep out water.

_____ **1.** Beavers are almost always
      A. playing   **C.** sleeping
      B. working   **D.** fighting

_____ **2.** A beaver home is called a
      A. cabin   **C.** lodge
      B. dam   **D.** ledge

_____ **3.** Beavers build dams across quiet
      A. puddles   **C.** streets
      B. oceans   **D.** streams

_____ **4.** Beavers cut down trees with their
      A. paws   **C.** saws
      B. teeth   **D.** tails

_____ **5.** Beavers pack the branches in their dams with
      A. clay   **C.** glue
      B. water   **D.** mud

The beaver's dam holds back the water in the stream. A pond forms behind the dam. Then the beaver builds its lodge in the middle of the pond. This is the beaver's way of keeping its home safe from other animals.

Most of a beaver's lodge is under the water. The beaver dives under the water to get to the entrance. Then it swims through tunnels to get to the upper part of the lodge. This part of the lodge is above the water. It is a safe place where the beaver can raise a family.

The inside of a beaver's lodge is hollow. Here the beavers raise a family. They have as many as six young in April or May. Young beavers stay with their parents until they are two years old. Then they leave the lodge to find a new stream and begin their busy adult lives.

_____ **6.** Beavers build homes in the middle of ponds for
    A. fun   **C.** protest
    B. protection   **D.** enjoyment

_____ **7.** The entrance is
    A. very large   **C.** under the water
    B. under the ground   **D.** above the water

_____ **8.** The beaver swims through the entrance into
    A. stairs   **C.** tunnels
    B. mines   **D.** enemies

_____ **9.** The upper part of the lodge is
    A. on the banks   **C.** under the water
    B. behind the water   **D.** out of the water

_____ **10.** Beavers have as many as
    A. six young   **C.** eight young
    B. seven young   **D.** ten young

Ferris's Wheel

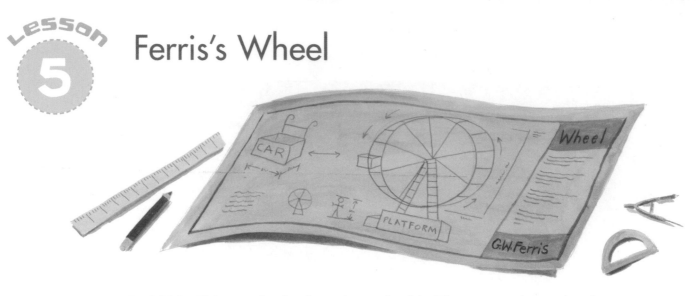

In 1892, Chicago city leaders planned a fair. They wanted it to be the greatest fair ever. It would show the newest ideas in science, business, and art. They also wanted to build something grand at the fair. The Eiffel Tower had been built three years before in France. The Chicago leaders wanted something even grander. So they asked people to send in designs.

G. W. Ferris was a young engineer. He heard about the fair. He designed a huge wheel made of steel. The wheel was 250 feet across. Large cars hung from the end of each spoke. Each car could carry 60 people in a giant circle through the air.

On May 1, 1893, the fair opened. People came from around the world to see the latest inventions. They felt the heat of new electric stoves. They stood in the cool breeze of small fans. They even saw a machine that washed dishes.

_____ **1.** Ferris's wheel was
- **A.** 1 mile high
- **B.** 250 feet across
- **C.** 250 yards across
- **D.** 60 feet tall

_____ **2.** Ferris's wheel was made of
- **A.** steel
- **B.** rubber
- **C.** wood
- **D.** gold

_____ **3.** Ferris designed his wheel so people could
- **A.** walk under it
- **B.** study it
- **C.** ride it
- **D.** learn about motion

_____ **4.** The fair opened
- **A.** in 1492
- **B.** in 1892
- **C.** in 1893
- **D.** in 1983

_____ **5.** People at the fair felt the heat of
- **A.** a bonfire
- **B.** gas heaters
- **C.** a heated fountain
- **D.** electric stoves

Ferris's wheel was the main attraction at the Chicago fair. People stood in line to ride on it. They wanted to see the fairgrounds from the wheel's highest point. As the wheel cranked upward, some people were frightened. Others were thrilled at what they saw below. Fountains glistened in the sunlight. Flags waved in the breeze. A train snaked through the grounds. At night colored searchlights lit the sky. Their beams reflected off the water fountains.

When the fair closed, the newspapers called it "a splendid fantasy." Ferris's wheel was later sold for scrap. Today smaller wheels based on his idea turn at fairs all over America. They are called Ferris wheels.

_____ **6.** Ferris's wheel was an attraction

    A. in France   **C.** in Chicago

    B. in Columbus   **D.** beside the Eiffel Tower

_____ **7.** Ferris's wheel

    A. broke down   **C.** was dangerous

    B. was popular   **D.** came from France

_____ **8.** People who rode Ferris's wheel could see

    A. the Eiffel Tower   **C.** Canada

    B. France   **D.** fountains and flags

_____ **9.** Newspapers called the fair a

    A. disaster   **C.** fantasy

    B. failure   **D.** thrill

_____ **10.** Ferris's wheel was sold for scrap

    A. after the fair   **C.** in 1892

    B. before the fair   **D.** during the fair

Starfish

Starfish of different sizes and colors live in the oceans. Starfish are often yellow, orange, or brown. They can be other colors, too. From point to point, a starfish can be as small as a paper clip or as long as a yardstick. Most starfish are shaped like stars, with five arms extending from their bodies. Some starfish, called sunstars, have a dozen arms. Other types have 25 arms.

Rows of tiny spines cover the top of a starfish's arms. Each spine moves easily when it is touched. Enemies that brush against a starfish may get a surprise. Some starfish spines are very sharp and have poison in them.

Underneath each arm of a starfish are rows of tiny holes. Tube feet extend from these holes. The tube feet can become suction cups to help starfish grip things. These suction cups hold starfish very strongly. Even storm waves will not tear a starfish from a rock.

_____ **1.** Starfish are often
    A. red   **C.** blue
    B. yellow   **D.** green

_____ **2.** From point to point, a starfish can be the size of a
    A. grain of rice   **C.** yardstick
    B. car   **D.** door

_____ **3.** A starfish can protect itself with its
    A. tube feet   **C.** mouth
    B. arms   **D.** spines

_____ **4.** The tube feet of a starfish are located
    A. on its back   **C.** under suction cups
    B. near its mouth   **D.** underneath its arms

_____ **5.** The suction-cup feet of a starfish
    A. are weak   **C.** are very strong
    B. have bristles   **D.** have pointed tips

A starfish's mouth is on its underside. It is in the middle of its body. Starfish swallow small animals whole. Sometimes they eat mollusks. These include clams and oysters, which are protected by hard shells. A starfish attaches its tube feet to each side of the shell. Then it slowly pries the shell open. The starfish next pushes its stomach out through its mouth, into the open shell. There, its stomach begins to digest the soft flesh.

Fishers who collect oysters and clams sometimes try to kill starfish by cutting them into pieces. This does not kill them. Starfish can grow new arms. They can even grow a new body. This can happen when one arm remains attached to a piece of the old body. Even a small part of a starfish's body can become another starfish.

_____ **6.** A starfish's mouth is
    A. on one arm   **C.** on its tube feet
    B. inside its stomach   **D.** on its underside

_____ **7.** Starfish swallow
    A. small animals   **C.** plants
    B. other starfish   **D.** tiny spines

_____ **8.** Oysters and clams are
    A. mammals   **C.** reptiles
    B. seashells   **D.** mollusks

_____ **9.** An oyster has
    A. a shell   **C.** arms
    B. a clam   **D.** spines

_____ **10.** If a starfish loses an arm, it will
    A. die   **C.** grow another
    B. not move   **D.** lose another

Ed's Dream Garden

Ed lives right outside a small town. He has decided to turn his back yard into a water garden with ponds and waterfalls. He wants flowers to grow everywhere, even in the ponds. Because Ed does not know how to begin, he signs up for a tour with his neighbor, Mr. Hall. Mr. Hall is known for his water gardens. He gives tours each Saturday.

On Saturday Mr. Hall greets Ed and takes him through a gate to his gardens. They pass a pond covered with large, green leaves floating on top of the water. Mr. Hall calls them lily pads. To Ed they look like big stepping-stones. Mr. Hall tells Ed about a type of water lily in South America with even bigger leaves. Its leaves can be more than 5 feet across. Mr. Hall explains that the plant is called the Victoria lily. Its leaves look like giant green pie pans because their edges turn up.

_____ **1.** Ed and Mr. Hall live
    A. in different states   **C.** on different farms
    B. in the same area   **D.** in a large city

_____ **2.** Mr. Hall gives tours
    A. every day   **C.** on Saturdays
    B. on Mondays   **D.** once a month

_____ **3.** To Ed the lily pads look like
    A. green frogs   **C.** pie pans
    B. stones to walk on   **D.** waterfalls

_____ **4.** The Victoria lily
    A. has enormous leaves   **C.** grows on land
    B. has purple berries   **D.** blooms each Saturday

_____ **5.** The Victoria lily's leaves look like pie pans because of their
    A. size   **C.** name
    B. color   **D.** shape

Ed sees blue flowers scattered among the leaves. The blooms stand above the water on stout stalks. Each one has several petals attached to the stem. Mr. Hall explains that these Australian water lilies bloom all day. Other types of water lilies bloom only at night. He also explains that water lilies are not always blue. They can be yellow, pink, or red.

Ed asks if the plants have roots like other flowers. Mr. Hall explains how lilies grow. He says that the fruit of each water lily is like a berry. The berries are filled with seeds. Often the fruit ripens underwater. Then the seeds float away or sink. The roots of the plants grow from the seeds.

When Ed leaves, he thanks Mr. Hall. He tells Mr. Hall that he will plant water lilies in his garden. Mr. Hall shakes Ed's hand and offers to help him. He starts by giving Ed a package of seeds.

_____ **6.** The bloom that Ed sees is
    A. blue   **C.** red
    B. yellow   **D.** pink

_____ **7.** Australian water lilies
    A. make vines   **C.** bloom all day
    B. are white   **D.** don't have roots

_____ **8.** The fruit of each water lily is like a
    A. flower   **C.** stalk
    B. berry   **D.** seed

_____ **9.** The fruit of a water lily ripens
    A. in the mud   **C.** in the spring
    B. near the petals **D.** underwater

_____**10.** When Ed leaves, Mr. Hall gives him
    A. stems   **C.** seeds
    B. roots   **D.** flowers

Trail Drives

Millions of cattle roamed on the open range in the Old West. Cattle ranchers rounded them up. They could sell them in Texas for $4 or $5 each. Easterners also liked to eat beef. They would pay from $40 to $50 each. Cattle ranchers hired cowboys to drive their cattle north. In towns like Abilene and Dodge City, the railroads crossed the plains. There the cattle were put on trains headed for the East Coast.

Before each trail drive, several ranchers hired a leader for the long trip. This trail boss hired from 10 to 12 cowboys to round up the cattle. While the roundup was going on, the trail boss hired a wrangler and a cook. The wrangler gathered 50 or more horses for the trip. The cook prepared the chuck wagon for cooking beans, bacon, and biscuits on the trail.

_____ 1. A cow could be sold in Texas for
    A. $10   **C.** $40
    B. $4   **D.** $50

_____ 2. Cattle were driven
    A. east   **C.** north
    B. west   **D.** south

_____ 3. Cattle were taken to the East Coast on
    A. horses   **C.** wagons
    B. trains   **D.** trucks

_____ 4. The leader of a trail drive was called a
    A. trail boss   **C.** cook
    B. wrangler   **D.** roundup

_____ 5. Before the trail drive, the cook prepared the
    A. horses   **C.** cattle
    B. saddles   **D.** chuck wagon

Each trail drive lasted for two or three months. The cowboys drove the cattle as far as 1,000 miles. They moved from 2,000 to 3,000 cattle on each drive. Those who were new to the job rode behind the herd. The dust clogged their throats and burned their eyes. At night some cowboys circled the herd, often singing to pass the time. Others slept next to saddled horses, ready for action.

Cowboys faced thieves, storms, and unfriendly tribes on trail drives. They feared stampedes the most. If a single cow was startled and ran, all the others followed. The earth shook with a deafening roar under their pounding hooves. After one stampede, the restless cattle were easily scared into stampeding again. Cowboys knew that they couldn't stop a stampeding herd, but they rode in front of it and tried to turn the cattle into a circle. This did not always help. Herds sometimes ran for days.

_____ **6.** Trail drives lasted two or three
      A. days   **C.** months
      B. years   **D.** weeks

_____ **7.** At times the number of cattle on a drive was
      A. 12   **C.** 1,000
      B. 50   **D.** 3,000

_____ **8.** On the trail new cowboys were positioned
      A. in front of the herd   **C.** next to the herd
      B. behind the herd   **D.** among the herd

_____ **9.** On the trail a cowboy slept ready for
      A. rain   **C.** coffee
      B. action   **D.** a bath

_____ **10.** Stampedes were caused by
      A. horses   **C.** a frightened animal
      B. a sick animal   **D.** singing cowboys

Writing Roundup

Read the story below. Think about the facts. Then answer the questions in complete sentences.

Do you know how the sandwich got its name? The name comes from the man who invented it. In the 1700s there lived a man who belonged to the royal class of England. He was called the earl of Sandwich. One day he was too busy to stop for a meal. He asked his servant to bring him two slices of bread and some roast meat. He placed the meat between the bread slices. The first sandwich was invented! The earl named the creation after himself.

1. Who invented the sandwich?

_____

_____

2. When was the sandwich invented?

_____

_____

3. What was the first sandwich made of?

_____

_____

Prewriting

Think of an idea you might write about, such as an important invention or a well-known person. Write the idea in the center of the idea web below. Then fill out the rest of the web with facts.

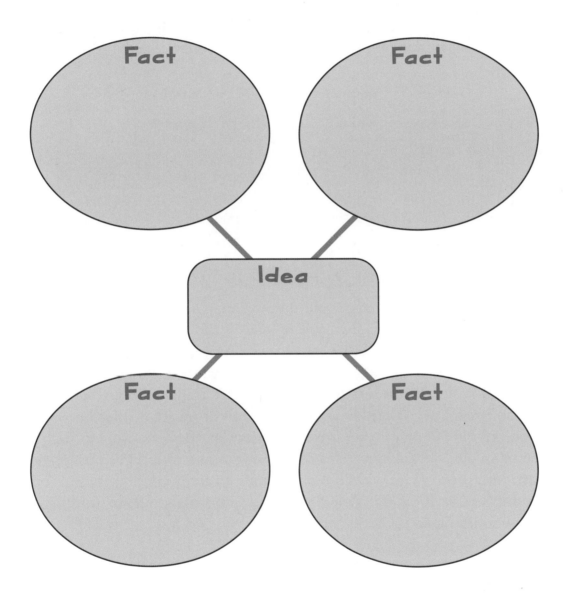

On Your Own

Now use another sheet of paper to write a paragraph about your idea. Use the facts from your idea web.

What Is Sequence?

Sequence means time order, or 1-2-3 order. If several things happen in a story, they happen in a sequence. One event happens first, and it is followed by another event.

You can find the sequence of events in a story by looking for *time words*, such as *first*, *next*, and *last*. Here is a list of time words:

later	during	days of the week
today	while	months of the year

Try It!

Here is a paragraph that tells a story. See if you can follow the sequence. Circle all the time words.

John Muir

Many people try to protect nature now, but 100 years ago, few people thought about it. John Muir helped to change that. Muir was born in Scotland. Later he moved with his family to a farm in Wisconsin. He loved nature. He also loved to invent things. In 1867, an accident almost cost him an eye. Muir gave up inventing. That same year he began a 1,000-mile walk to the Gulf of Mexico. Later he wrote a book about the plants and animals he saw. In 1868, he went to the Yosemite Valley in California. He spent six years exploring this part of the West. Muir became convinced that the government needed to save areas of great beauty. In 1890, Muir persuaded Congress to set up Yosemite and Sequoia National Parks. In 1892, he founded the Sierra Club.

Try putting these events in the order that they happened. What happened first? Write the number **1** on the line by that sentence. Write the number **2** by the sentence that tells what happened next. Write the number **3** by the sentence that tells what happened last.

_____ Muir explored the Yosemite Valley.

_____ Muir moved to Wisconsin.

_____ Congress set up two national parks.

Practice with Sequence

This unit asks questions about sequence in stories. Here are some practice questions. The first two are already answered. You can do the third one on your own.

__B__ 1. When was the Sierra Club founded?
   A. before Muir went on the 1,000-mile walk
   B. after Yosemite became a national park
   C. while Muir was an inventor

Look at the question. It has the words *Sierra Club* and *founded*. Find those words in the story. You will find the sentence, "In 1892, he founded the Sierra Club." The sentence before this one says that Muir persuaded Congress to set up Yosemite and Sequoia National Parks in 1890. So B is the correct answer. Muir founded the Sierra Club two years after Yosemite became a national park.

__C__ 2. What happened just before Muir walked to the Gulf of Mexico?
   A. he wrote a book about what he saw
   B. he grew up on a farm
   C. he almost lost an eye

Look at the question carefully. Notice the time word *before*. Notice also that the word *just* is there. So the question is asking what happened *just before* Muir walked to the Gulf of Mexico. In the story you will find these sentences: "In 1867, an accident almost cost him an eye. Muir gave up inventing. That same year he began a 1,000-mile walk to the Gulf of Mexico." So the correct answer is C.

_____ 3. When did Muir persuade Congress to set up Yosemite and Sequoia National Parks?
   A. when he was exploring Yosemite
   B. before he walked to the Gulf of Mexico
   C. in 1890

Can you find the answer?

Read each story. After each story you will answer questions about the sequence of events in the story. Remember, sequence is the order of things.

Garden Art

Is it a tree? Is it a bear? If you're looking at a tree in the shape of a bear, it's a topiary. A topiary is a tree or bush that is trained into a shape. Topiaries are a kind of sculpture. Growing a topiary garden takes both time and skill.

The first thing a topiary gardener does is make a drawing. The drawing shows the form the gardener would like a tree or bush to take. The gardener then chooses the bush for the topiary. It may be one that was just planted or one that is already in place. Special bushes are used for topiaries. These bushes are yew, privet, or boxwood.

In June of the plant's first year, the gardener looks for new leaves. When the leaves grow, it is time to shape the bottom of the bush. The gardener shapes the bottom of the bush for about five years. The top is not trimmed during this time.

In the fifth year, the bush grows tall enough for shaping. Then the gardener begins to shape the whole bush. Sometimes branches are bent to form a shape. The gardener wires the branches in place.

Once a topiary has been started, it needs care all year. In the summer it must be clipped many times to keep its shape. This cutting also helps the bush grow. In the winter the bushes don't grow. The gardeners have to brush snow off the plants. Snow can hurt the flat parts of the plants.

Topiary gardening is a very old art. The Romans did it in the first century. In the sixteenth century, people in Europe liked topiaries too. The Dutch and French grew very pretty topiaries in their neat gardens. By the late 1600s, topiaries were also grown in America. Today there is a topiary garden in Williamsburg, Virginia. It's much like a garden that grew there hundreds of years ago.

1. Put these events in the order that they happened. What happened first? Write the number **1** on the line by that sentence. Then write the number **2** by the sentence that tells what happened next. Write the number **3** by the sentence that tells what happened last.

_____ The gardener chooses the bush.

_____ The gardener draws a sketch.

_____ The gardener shapes the bottom of the bush.

_____ 2. When does the gardener look for new growth?
   A. in the fifth year
   B. in June
   C. after the first century

_____ 3. How long does it take a topiary bush to grow tall enough for shaping?
   A. five years
   B. hundreds of years
   C. one year

_____ 4. When did the Romans grow topiaries?
   A. in the late 1600s
   B. in the first century
   C. in the fifth century

_____ 5. When were topiaries first grown in America?
   A. before the 1500s
   B. during the 1600s
   C. after the 1700s

Football Factory

A football has to be tough. After all, it gets kicked around most of the time. Each football is made very carefully. It takes about 50 steps to make a football.

It all starts with leather. About 2 feet of leather are needed to cover a pro football. A machine cuts the leather into four pieces. Another machine stamps the pieces. The stamp tells the name of the company that makes the ball. Workers then sew a cloth lining to each piece. Next they stitch the four pieces together. A small opening is left. The football is then turned inside out. Workers trim the extra leather inside.

The football is turned right side out again. A worker puts a rubber lining into the ball. Now the opening in the ball is sewed up. Each ball is sewed three times by hand. The first time, a worker uses heavy linen thread to close the opening. After that, two sets of leather laces are added. These laces help players get a good grip on the ball.

Once the ball is sewed up, it is placed on an iron mold. A worker pumps air into the rubber lining. Then another worker shines the leather football.

Next workers weigh and measure the ball to see that it is the right size and the right weight. A football should weigh between 14 and 15 ounces. It should be 21 inches around and 11 inches from end to end. A good football must be strong so it stands up to rough play. It must not be too hard or players will hurt their feet when they kick it.

If the football is just right, it goes to the packing area. Workers then put the balls in boxes to send to professional teams and sports stores.

1. Put these events in the order that they happened. What happened first? Write the number **1** on the line by that sentence. Then write the number **2** by the sentence that tells what happened next. Write the number **3** by the sentence that tells what happened last.

_____ Machines cut pieces from leather.

_____ Workers sew in a cloth lining.

_____ Machines stamp the leather pieces.

_____ **2.** When are the four pieces sewed together?
    A. while a worker sews in a cloth lining
    B. before the inside is trimmed
    C. after workers check the ball's weight

_____ **3.** When is a rubber lining put into the football?
    A. while the ball is turned inside out
    B. after the ball is turned right side out
    C. before the ball is turned inside out

_____ **4.** When is each ball sewed up with leather laces?
    A. before the rubber lining is added
    B. while the lining is added
    C. after it is sewed with linen thread

_____ **5.** When are the footballs measured?
    A. after they are sent to stores
    B. while they are inspected
    C. while they are used in games

Making Skeletons

Some people make skeletons for a living. Here are the bare-bones facts.

At a factory in England, workers make human skeletons from plastic. The skeletons are sold to hospitals and schools that train doctors. They are sent to more than 40 countries around the world. People study the skeletons to learn about the human body. Some scientists think these plastic skeletons are better and last longer than the real ones.

The workers start with a soft plastic called acrylic. They pour the acrylic into molds. It takes two hours for the acrylic to get hard. Then the workers remove the plastic bones from the molds. The factory has more than 200 molds. That is one mold for each bone in the body.

The next job is to smooth any rough spots on the bones. The workers polish these rough spots with power tools. The finished bones are then placed in special drawers. There is a drawer for each kind of bone.

Next it's time to put the bones together. Each worker puts together a different part of the body. For instance, one person puts together the hands. Each hand has 30 different small bones in it. The worker drills a tiny hole in each bone. Thin wire is then slipped into the holes. The wire holds the bones together in the right position.

Another worker puts together the rib cage. The ribs are made of rubber so they can be bent. Then they are wired together to form a rib cage. The worker joins the rib cage to the spine.

Finally all the skeleton parts are put together. The finished skeleton is hung up on a rack. An expert checks to make sure all the bones are in place. At the week's end, about 20 skeletons are ready for shipment.

1. Put these events in the order that they happened. What happened first? Write the number **1** on the line by that sentence. Then write the number **2** by the sentence that tells what happened next. Write the number **3** by the sentence that tells what happened last.

_____ People study plastic skeletons.

_____ People make plastic skeletons.

_____ Skeletons are sold to hospitals.

_____ **2.** When do workers place the bones in drawers?
    A. after they are smoothed over
    B. before the acrylic is hard
    C. before they are smoothed over

_____ **3.** When are hand bones wired together?
    A. after a worker drills holes in them
    B. while the acrylic gets hard
    C. after they are shipped around the world

_____ **4.** When do workers smooth the bones?
    A. after they arc put in drawers
    B. after workers remove bones from molds
    C. after workers put the bones together

_____ **5.** When is the skeleton hung on a rack?
    A. after the bones are joined together
    B. after an expert checks it
    C. before the bones are placed in drawers

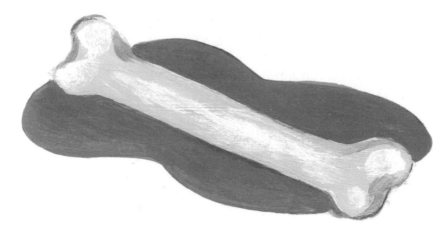

The post office has plenty of work to do. It handles thousands of letters per day. Let's follow a letter all the way across America.

Juan lives in New York. He wrote a letter to Dave. Dave lives in Oregon. Juan put the letter in the mailbox on Monday night. On Tuesday morning a truck stopped at the mailbox. The mail carrier put the letters into a large bag and took the bag to a post office in New York.

Tuesday afternoon the letters were sorted. Zip codes were used to sort the mail. A machine picked up a letter and held it. A worker read the Zip code. Then the worker pushed five buttons on another machine. The worker had only one second to do this. After the worker pushed the buttons, the machine put the letter in a box. By Tuesday night the box was on a truck. The truck went to the airport. An airplane took off for Oregon on Wednesday morning. Juan's letter went on the airplane.

By noon the letters were in an airport in Oregon. Mail trucks then took them to post offices. One of these was in Dave's town. Wednesday night people in Dave's town sorted the letters by street name.

Thursday morning the mail carrier for Main Street picked up her pile of letters. She sorted all of them by street address. The people at 1 Main Street got their mail first. Dave lived at 221 Main Street. He got his letter before lunch.

1. Put these events in the order that they happened. What happened first? Write the number **1** on the line by that sentence. Then write the number **2** by the sentence that tells what happened next. Write the number **3** by the sentence that tells what happened last.

_____ The machine put the letter in a box.

_____ A worker read the Zip code.

_____ A worker pushed five buttons.

_____ **2.** Where did Juan's letter travel first?
    A. on a truck that went to the airport
    B. to a post office in New York
    C. to a post office in Oregon

_____ **3.** When did the letter go to Oregon?
    A. Monday night
    B. Wednesday morning
    C. Tuesday morning

_____ **4.** When did people sort the letters by street names?
    A. before the letters went on the airplane
    B. Wednesday night
    C. Tuesday night

_____ **5.** When did Dave get the letter?
    A. Monday after lunch
    B. Tuesday afternoon
    C. Thursday before lunch

The Digestive System

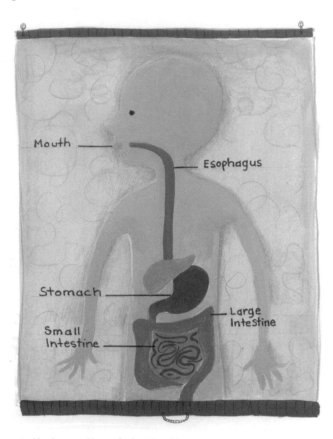

Have you ever wondered what happens to the food you eat? Most people know that food provides energy for the body. Do you know how food becomes energy? We can find out by studying the digestive system.

Digestion is the breaking down of food into nutrients. Nutrients are the parts of food that the body can use. The nutrients must be small enough so that the blood can carry them to all the cells of the body.

The first part of the digestive system is the mouth. Food enters the body through the mouth. Teeth grind up the food into small pieces. The food is mixed with a liquid called saliva.

Saliva has a chemical that changes starch into sugar. This is the first step in breaking down food. When you swallow, food goes down the esophagus. This long tube leads into the stomach.

In the stomach more chemicals are mixed with the food. More starches are changed into sugar. Stomach juices begin to break down proteins. The muscles of the stomach act like a blender to turn the food into liquid.

When food leaves the stomach, it goes into the small intestine. The small intestine is like a hose. If it were stretched out, it would be 20 feet long. Blood vessels line the walls of the small intestine. These blood vessels soak up the nutrients. Then the blood carries the nutrients to every cell in the body.

The food that is left is not needed by the body. It passes into the large intestine. From there it is carried out of the body.

1. Put these events in the order that they happened. What happened first? Write the number **1** on the line by that sentence. Then write the number **2** by the sentence that tells what happened next. Write the number **3** by the sentence that tells what happened last.

_____ The food that is left goes into the large intestine.

_____ Chemicals mix with food in the stomach.

_____ Teeth grind up the food into small pieces.

_____ **2.** When is food mixed with saliva?
    A. while it is in the stomach
    B. when it is in the mouth
    C. after it is in the small intestine

_____ **3.** When does food go down the esophagus?
    A. after you swallow
    B. after it leaves the stomach
    C. when it leaves the large intestine

_____ **4.** When do juices begin to break down proteins?
    A. when food is in the mouth
    B. after food is in the small intestine
    C. while food is in the stomach

_____ **5.** Where do blood vessels soak up the nutrients?
    A. in the small intestine
    B. in the large intestine
    C. in the stomach

Koalas

Koalas are sometimes called koala bears because they look like live teddy bears. But koalas aren't bears. They are marsupials. Marsupials are mammals with pouches. Most marsupials live in Australia. If you lived in Australia, you could go to a koala preserve and see these cute, cuddly animals for yourself.

After mating, a female koala waits for about five weeks. Then her tiny, blind baby is born. The hairless baby is about 3/4 of an inch long. It looks like a worm with a big head and arms. The baby koala must climb 6 inches to get into its mother's pouch. This is a dangerous journey. If the tiny koala falls off, it will die.

The baby is safe once it's inside the mother's pouch. A strong muscle keeps the pouch closed for the first few months. The baby has plenty to eat. It grows larger, and its fur becomes thick. From time to time, it sticks its head out and looks around.

The baby stays in the pouch for about six months. Then it is ready to come out for short periods of time. By now it is 7 inches long and has its first teeth. The baby chews on young gum leaves, and drinks its mother's milk.

After leaving the pouch, the koala baby rides on its mother's back. The mother's strong arms and claws allow her to climb easily, even with the baby on her back. For the next few months, the baby clings to its mother during the day. At night it returns to the pouch. At about nine months old, the young koala will go short distances from the mother to eat gum leaves by itself.

The mother koala takes good care of her baby for about a year. By then the baby is full grown and can take care of itself.

1. Put these events in the order that they happened. What happened first? Write the number **1** on the line by that sentence. Then write the number **2** by the sentence that tells what happened next. Write the number **3** by the sentence that tells what happened last.

_____ The baby koala stays in the pouch for six months.

_____ The tiny, blind baby is born.

_____ The baby koala rides on its mother's back.

_____ **2.** When does the baby koala look like a worm?
    A. when it's about six months old
    B. after it's a year old
    C. when it's born

_____ **3.** When does the baby koala make a dangerous journey?
    A. when it first tries to reach its mother's pouch
    B. the first time it climbs a tree
    C. when it's 18 months old

_____ **4.** When does the baby koala first leave the pouch?
    A. before it's five weeks old
    B. when it's about six months old
    C. after it's full grown

_____ **5.** How long does a mother koala care for her baby?
    A. about one year
    B. less than six weeks
    C. more than three years

Have you ever seen a huge, cigar-shaped balloon called a blimp, or airship? They are sometimes used for advertising. Blimps float because they are filled with a gas that is lighter than air. They have engines and can be steered.

In the 1930s blimps were used for passenger travel. The *Hindenburg* was one of the largest airships ever built. It had made 10 trips from Germany to the United States. On May 3, 1937, it left Frankfurt to make another trip across the Atlantic. There were 97 people on board.

The *Hindenburg* was filled with hydrogen. Hydrogen explodes easily. For this reason passengers were not allowed to carry matches or lighters. People wore shoes with rubber soles to prevent sparks. Many safety measures were taken to prevent a fire.

On May 6 the *Hindenburg* neared Lakehurst, New Jersey. This is where it would land. Passengers gathered their luggage. They waved to friends and families waiting below. Just then Captain Pruss felt a jolt. He wondered what it was. He heard screaming on the field below. On his radio someone cried, "The ship is burning!"

People watching from below were terrified. The tail of the ship had burst into flames. The ship was crashing to the ground. Some passengers jumped out the windows. The ground crew ran for their lives.

The fire caused 36 deaths. No one knew what caused the ship to explode. Perhaps it was static electricity. There was no way to tell for certain. After the crash of the *Hindenburg*, airships were never again used for passenger travel.

1. Put these events in the order that they happened. What happened first? Write the number **1** on the line by that sentence. Then write the number **2** by the sentence that tells what happened next. Write the number **3** by the sentence that tells what happened last.

_____ The *Hindenburg* neared Lakehurst, New Jersey.

_____ Airships were never again used for passenger travel.

_____ The *Hindenburg* burst into flames.

_____ **2.** When were airships used for passenger travel?
    A. before balloons were invented
    B. in the 1930s
    C. after the *Hindenburg* crashed

_____ **3.** When did the *Hindenburg* leave Frankfurt?
    A. in the spring of 1937
    B. after the winter of 1940
    C. before the summer of 1935

_____ **4.** When did the *Hindenburg* crash?
    A. on November 1
    B. on April 5
    C. on May 6

_____ **5.** When did Captain Pruss feel a jolt?
    A. before they left Frankfurt
    B. while they were getting ready to land
    C. as soon as they saw the Atlantic Ocean

Great Blue Whales

Blue whales are the largest animals that have ever lived. The tongue of a blue whale can weigh as much as a small elephant. Blue whales can weigh 150 tons and can be 100 feet long. Even though they are huge, blue whales are graceful. They swim fast and make quick turns.

There used to be hundreds of thousands of these giants in the oceans. For many years, they were killed for their meat and blubber. Now most countries have agreed to stop hunting these whales. No one knows for sure how many blue whales are left.

Instead of teeth blue whales have a baleen that looks like a large comb. The blue whale eats small, shrimplike animals called krill. The blue whale opens its mouth to let in water and krill. Then it closes its mouth and forces the water out. The baleen keeps the krill inside. In Antarctica there are so many krill the ocean looks orange. A hungry blue whale can eat 8,000 pounds of krill per day.

Female whales are called cows. Their babies are called calves. Blue whales give birth to their babies in warm waters. Blue whale calves grow faster than any other animal. They gain about 200 pounds per day for the first seven months.

In the spring when the calf is a few months old, the mother and baby begin migrating. They swim south to Antarctica to find food. For about six months, the mother whale has not had much to eat. The baby has been living on its mother's milk. The baby and mother travel alone. It takes the two whales many weeks to reach Antarctica.

When fall comes the young whale is old enough and large enough to take care of itself. It will make the return trip to warm waters alone. In a few years, it will look for a mate.

1. Put these events in the order that they happened. What happened first? Write the number **1** on the line by that sentence. Then write the number **2** by the sentence that tells what happened next. Write the number **3** by the sentence that tells what happened last.

_____ Countries agreed to stop hunting blue whales.

_____ Blue whales were hunted for their meat and blubber.

_____ There once were hundreds of thousands of blue whales.

_____ **2.** When do blue whales migrate to Antarctica?
    A. before the calf is born
    B. when the calf is a few months old
    C. during a full moon

_____ **3.** How long does it take the whales to get to Antarctica?
    A. many weeks
    B. a few days
    C. many months

_____ **4.** When do blue whale calves gain 200 pounds per day?
    A. before they are born
    B. when they look for a mate
    C. during the first seven months of their lives

_____ **5.** When is the young blue whale old enough to take care of itself?
    A. when it weighs 100 tons
    B. when fall comes
    C. soon after it is born

Writing Roundup

Read the paragraph below. Think about the sequence, or time order.
Answer the questions in complete sentences.

What happens when you ride in an elevator? First, two sets of doors close and lock. One set is in the walls of the building, and the other set is part of the elevator car. Next a motor turns on. Then cables pull the car up. While the car goes up, a set of weights goes down to balance the load. When the car reaches the chosen floor, brakes hold the car in place. The doors open, and people can get out.

1. When you ride in an elevator, what happens first?

_____

_____

2. What happens while cables pull the car up?

_____

_____

3. What happens when the car reaches the chosen floor?

_____

_____

4. What happens last when you ride in an elevator?

_____

_____

Prewriting

Think about something that you have done, such as eating at a restaurant, baking a loaf of bread, or playing a game of checkers. Write the events in sequence below.

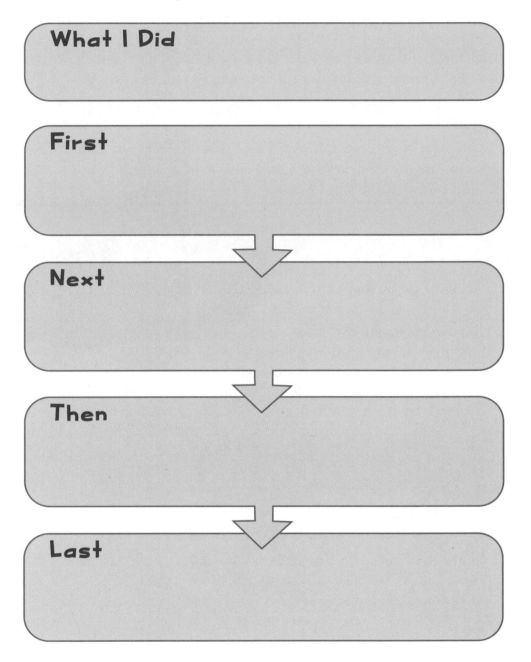

What I Did

First

Next

Then

Last

On Your Own

Now use another sheet of paper to write a paragraph about what you have done. Write the events in the order that they happened. Use time order words.

What Is Context?

Context means all the words in a sentence or all the sentences in a paragraph. In a sentence all the words together make up the context. In a paragraph all the sentences together make up the context. You can use the context to figure out the meaning of unknown words.

Try It!

The following paragraph has a word that you may not know. See whether you can use the context (the sentences and other words in the paragraph) to find out what the word means.

It was midnight. Mr. Blake had been driving for a long time. He began to feel **drowsy**. His eyes fluttered shut, and his head nodded forward. He awoke with a jerk a second later. "It's time for me to stop driving," he thought. Mr. Blake pulled over at the next motel.

If you don't know what **drowsy** means, you can decide by using the context. The paragraph contains these words:

Clue: his eyes fluttered shut

Clue: his head nodded forward

Clue: he awoke

Find these clues in the paragraph and circle them. What words do you think of when you read the clues? You might think of *tired*. What other words do you think of? Write the words below:

_____

Did you write *sleepy*? The context clue words tell you that **drowsy** means "sleepy."

Working with Context

This unit asks questions that you can answer by using context clues in paragraphs. There are two kinds of paragraphs. The paragraphs in the first part of this unit have blank spaces in them. You can use the context clues in the paragraphs to decide which word should go in each space. Here is an example:

Elizabeth Blackwell was the first woman doctor in the United States. She tried to get into many ___**1**___ schools before she was finally accepted. Later she opened a hospital. It was run ___**2**___ by women.

___*B*___ 1. **A.** music   **B.** medical   **C.** beauty   **D.** special

_____ 2. **A.** entirely   **B.** darkly   **C.** softly   **D.** fast

Look at the answer words for question 1. Treat the paragraph as a puzzle. Which pieces don't fit? Which piece fits best? Try putting each word in the blank. See which one makes the most sense. Doctors don't go to *music* schools or *beauty* schools. Doctors do go to a *special* school. *Special* is a possible answer. But *medical* is even better. The correct answer is *medical*, answer **B**. Now try to answer question 2 on your own.

The paragraphs in the second part of this unit are different. For these you figure out the meaning of a word that is printed in **dark letters** in the paragraph. Here is an example:

Daffodils are a sign of spring. Their bright yellow color and long, thin leaves are easy to spot. Wild daffodils cover hillsides in the country. Other kinds are found in city parks.

The word in dark type is **daffodils**. Find the context clues. Then find the answer words that mean the same as **daffodils**.

_____ 3. In this paragraph, the word **daffodils** means
     A. a kind of bird   **C.** a kind of animal
     B. a kind of flower   **D.** a kind of kite

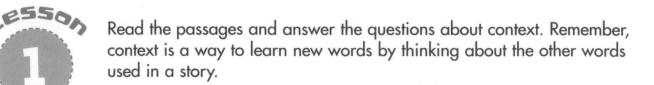

Read the passages and answer the questions about context. Remember, context is a way to learn new words by thinking about the other words used in a story.

Computers are fun and ____1____ machines. They help us store and work with information. Some people use them to ____2____ math problems. Others like them just for playing games.

_____ 1. **A.** lazy   **B.** helpless   **C.** useful   **D.** awkward

_____ 2. **A.** earn   **B.** solve   **C.** refuse   **D.** destroy

The cheetah is a big cat. It is known for its great speed as it runs short ____3____. It uses its sleek body and long, powerful legs to run fast. This cat's claws help it grab the ground as it races to catch its ____4____.

_____ 3. **A.** days   **B.** evenings   **C.** naps   **D.** stretches

_____ 4. **A.** bath   **B.** water   **C.** quarry   **D.** apple

Lightning is usually seen as a streak across the sky. Lightning in the shape of a ____5____ is called ball lightning. It is rarely seen, and no one can ____6____ why it occurs.

_____ 5. **A.** sphere   **B.** square   **C.** heart   **D.** line

_____ 6. **A.** deny   **B.** recall   **C.** explain   **D.** cure

A telescope is used to make ____7____ stars look closer and larger. It looks like a long tube. The light from a star enters one end of the tube. Two mirrors are used to ____8____ the light to an eyepiece. When you look through the eyepiece, you are able to get a better view of the star.

_____ 7. **A.** remote   **B.** narrow   **C.** late   **D.** wild

_____ 8. **A.** attach   **B.** brush   **C.** tow   **D.** reflect

The ostrich is the largest bird in the world. It can grow to a height of 8 feet and can weigh 300 __**9**__. The ostrich can't fly, but it can run fast to __**10**__ from danger.

_____ **9.** **A.** pounds   **B.** miles   **C.** bikes   **D.** insects

_____ **10.** **A.** remove   **B.** escape   **C.** walk   **D.** block

---

The tiger lives in parts of Asia. It is the largest __**11**__ of the cat family. Its fur is brownish orange with black stripes. The tiger __**12**__ the woods alone as it hunts for large prey to eat.

_____ **11.** **A.** food   **B.** member   **C.** country   **D.** enemy

_____ **12.** **A.** prowls   **B.** eats   **C.** obeys   **D.** sleeps

---

The abacus is a counting __**13**__. It was invented thousands of years ago. It has beads strung on wires that are attached to a frame. The beads are used to represent numbers. Math problems are __**14**__ by moving the beads.

_____ **13.** **A.** time   **B.** force   **C.** value   **D.** machine

_____ **14.** **A.** failed   **B.** calculated   **C.** avoided   **D.** melted

---

The castle was once a very important place, and it had many uses. It was a palace for the rulers of the region. Lawbreakers were held in a __**15**__ that was part of the castle. The castle also served as a __**16**__ for protection against enemies.

_____ **15.** **A.** tree   **B.** prison   **C.** closet   **D.** window

_____ **16.** **A.** fort   **B.** curtain   **C.** ranch   **D.** harvest

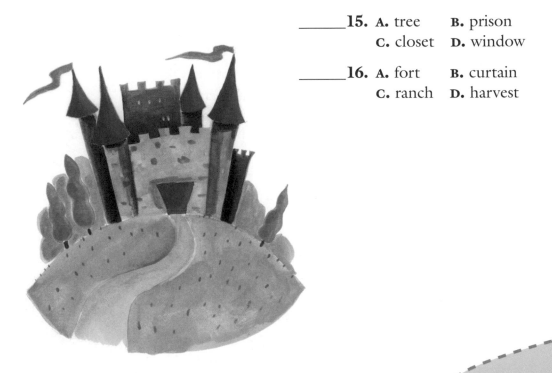

Stonehenge is a circle of huge stones. It stands on a flat ___1___ in England. It was ___2___ more than 4,000 years ago. It may have been used for measuring time. There are still many questions about how and why it was built.

_____ 1. **A.** hug   **B.** plain   **C.** river   **D.** carpet

_____ 2. **A.** delayed   **B.** taught   **C.** chased   **D.** erected

---

Although a koala looks similar to a bear, in ___3___ it is not a bear at all. This cute, cuddly ___4___ is a marsupial. This means a mother koala will carry her baby in a pouch as it grows.

_____ 3. **A.** object   **B.** fact   **C.** arm   **D.** hunger

_____ 4. **A.** bear   **B.** insect   **C.** creature   **D.** savage

---

You know that calculators are well ___5___ because so many people use them. This was not always the case. Calculators have gone through many ___6___. At first, calculators were large and solved problems slowly. Today they are much smaller and can compute problems quickly.

_____ 5. **A.** launched   **B.** poured   **C.** accepted   **D.** won

_____ 6. **A.** keys   **B.** books   **C.** parts   **D.** stages

---

What animal can eat 50 pounds of food in one sitting? If you said "elephant," you are right, but that little bit isn't dinner. It's more like a ___7___. Can you guess how much food an elephant eats in a day? If you said up to 500 pounds, you have an ___8___ idea of how much it eats.

_____ 7. **A.** drink   **B.** friend
        C. snack   **D.** foot

_____ 8. **A.** apple   **B.** engine
        C. accurate   **D.** ill

The first human-powered airplane crossed the English Channel in 1979. It looked like a bicycle enclosed in a cabin with long wings. It held just one person. The craft's only power came from the __9__ of a human. The __10__ pedaled to turn the propeller that was in the back of the plane.

_____ 9. A. muscles   B. eyes   C. nerves   D. thoughts

_____10. A. engine   B. pilot   C. wind   D. battery

Prairie dogs are small, furry animals. They love to play. They live in __11__ called towns. Prairie dogs build their __12__ by digging holes and tunnels.

_____11. A. houses   B. colonies
            C. toys   D. plants

_____12. A. cars   B. families
            C. hopes   D. burrows

People once used pools of water as mirrors. Then they saw that __13__, polished pieces of metal made better mirrors. Later, metallic film was __14__ to the back of polished plates of glass. This process made the best mirrors.

_____13. A. scratched   B. smooth   C. dark   D. heavy

_____14. A. summoned   B. led   C. applied   D. trotted

A sea horse is a tiny fish with a long tail. Its head looks like that of a horse. It moves by swimming upright. The sea horse has a single fin on its back that __15__ it through the water. If the sea horse wants to stop, it __16__ its tail around a sea plant.

_____15. A. lives   B. propels
            C. sings   D. feeds

_____16. A. coils   B. loses
            C. hits   D. plants

Geckos are lizards that are good climbers. There are more than 800 varieties of geckos. Many of them make clicking ___1___ with their tongues. Others are ___2___ and never make any noise.

_____ 1. **A.** eyes   **B.** bites   **C.** sounds   **D.** leaps

_____ 2. **A.** tan   **B.** tired   **C.** nervous   **D.** silent

---

Wind power is an old ___3___ of energy. The windmills used now are much better than they once were. Windmills can supply ___4___ power to run lights, toasters, fans, and radios in homes.

_____ 3. **A.** plan   **B.** job   **C.** trick   **D.** type

_____ 4. **A.** wave   **B.** electrical   **C.** solar   **D.** no

---

Flying squirrels have flaps of skin between their hind and front legs. These flaps can be used like a parachute. The squirrels leap from high branches and ___5___ their flaps of skin. Then they ___6___ through the air to lower branches.

_____ 5. **A.** tear   **B.** wrinkle   **C.** spread   **D.** forget

_____ 6. **A.** trot   **B.** soar   **C.** freeze   **D.** look

---

A hedgehog is an unusual animal. It snorts as it ___7___ for food at night. If it senses danger, the hedgehog will roll into a ball with its spines pointed out. During the day it stays safe in its nest. Sometimes it will ___8___ loudly as it sleeps.

_____ 7. **A.** eats   **B.** rummages
       C. melts   **D.** dresses

_____ 8. **A.** type   **B.** march
       C. snore   **D.** eat

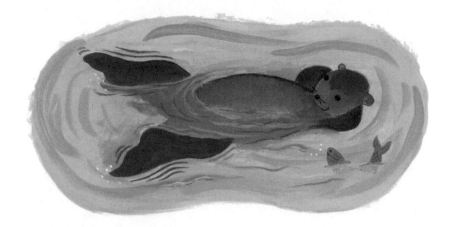

The sea otter can use a rock as a tool. First the otter __**9**__ in the water on its back. Then it puts a rock on its stomach. Finally the otter takes a clam and __**10**__ it against the rock to open it.

_____ **9.** **A.** writes   **B.** drifts   **C.** runs   **D.** covers

_____**10.** **A.** eats   **B.** rubs   **C.** smashes   **D.** fishes

Caribou are a type of large deer. The herds migrate long distances. They move across Greenland and the northern __**11**__ of North America. They eat many types of plants in open ranges when the weather is warm. At the first __**12**__ of winter, they start to move. They go to wooded regions. There they eat small plants. These plants grow on trees and under the snow.

_____**11.** **A.** echo   **B.** package   **C.** chain   **D.** territory

_____**12.** **A.** trails   **B.** indications   **C.** toes   **D.** cans

Riding in a hot-air balloon is quiet __**13**__ for the noise made by the gas burner. This burner is needed to __**14**__ a flame. The flame stretches up into the nylon or polyester bag. This bag is the balloon. The air inside the bag becomes lighter as it is warmed. This causes the balloon to rise. As the air inside the balloon cools, the balloon floats back down to the ground.

_____**13.** **A.** above   **B.** except   **C.** below   **D.** in

_____**14.** **A.** generate   **B.** brush   **C.** hug   **D.** surprise

A platypus is an odd animal. It is __**15**__ at ease on land or in the streams and lakes of Australia. The platypus swims to catch its food. The platypus uses its ducklike, __**16**__ front feet and its long, flat tail to swim. It sleeps in a burrow on shore.

_____**15.** **A.** tall   **B.** giant   **C.** equally   **D.** heavy

_____**16.** **A.** hot   **B.** webbed   **C.** tied   **D.** icy

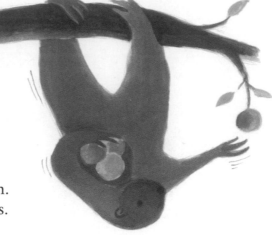

The sloth lives in the Central and South American forests. Its shaggy, grayish green hair helps it hide in the trees. The sloth has curved claws. It can hang upside down on a branch. It __1__ on fruit, leaves, and twigs. The sloth moves at a very slow pace. It drinks dew or raindrops when it is __2__ .

_____ 1. **A.** nibbles **B.** dances **C.** winks **D.** fixes

_____ 2. **A.** asleep **B.** tired **C.** brave **D.** thirsty

---

A rainbow is seen when the Sun's rays shine on drops of rain or mist. It appears in the sky __3__ the Sun. It has seven colors. The amount of space used by each color __4__ on the size of the waterdrops in the rainbow.

_____ 3. **A.** gold **B.** opposite **C.** water **D.** upset

_____ 4. **A.** quits **B.** blends **C.** sits **D.** depends

---

A hovercraft is a vehicle that __5__ on a layer of air above land or water. The air __6__ is made using fans. There is a rubber skirt on the craft's lower edge. It fills with air from the fans. This helps the craft cross rough ground or waves.

_____ 5. **A.** moves **B.** sews **C.** feeds **D.** crashes

_____ 6. **A.** show **B.** pill **C.** cushion **D.** stem

A sand dollar is an animal that lives in shallow waters off the coast. It stays partly __7__ in the sand. It crawls and digs using the little spines on its body. The sand dollar finds bits of food to eat while it digs in the __8__ of sand.

_____ 7. **A.** buried **B.** cut **C.** neat **D.** sewn

_____ 8. **A.** hearts **B.** tins **C.** grains **D.** castles

Long ago the giant panda was a common sight. It lived in many parts of China. Then people began cutting down ___9___ areas of bamboo. The giant panda had a hard time finding bamboo to eat. Now the giant panda lives only high in the mountains of southeastern China. People are working to protect the giant panda. Seeing a giant panda today is very ___10___.

_____ 9. **A.** easy   **B.** slight   **C.** dangerous   **D.** immense

_____10. **A.** purple   **B.** dry   **C.** uncommon   **D.** large

---

The first American woman to travel in space was Sally Ride. She went in the space shuttle for a six-day ___11___. Sally helped launch satellites, and she ___12___ experiments.

_____11. **A.** mission   **B.** sleep   **C.** leap   **D.** walk

_____12. **A.** obeyed   **B.** dyed   **C.** conducted   **D.** sealed

---

The manatee lives in freshwater canals. It's a mammal, but it spends its entire life in the water. The manatee helps keep the canals ___13___. It eats large amounts of plants that cause ___14___ in the canal.

_____13. **A.** happy   **B.** kind   **C.** clear   **D.** loud

_____14. **A.** blocks   **B.** signs   **C.** wagons   **D.** tables

---

A robot is a machine. It is built to do certain ___15___. A computer inside the robot gives it directions about how to complete special jobs. A robot is faster and makes fewer ___16___ than most people.

_____15. **A.** flips   **B.** tasks   **C.** flowers   **D.** calls

_____16. **A.** laws   **B.** sleeves   **C.** shouts   **D.** mistakes

Most people like football because it is full of action. But the ball is in motion only 20 percent of the game. The rest of the time is **expended** in things such as huddles and time-outs.

_____ **1.** In this paragraph, the word **expended** means

    A. kicked   **C.** wished

    B. spent   **D.** saved

You can measure yourself. On bare feet, stand with your back to a wall. Put a thin piece of cardboard across the top of your head and mark where it hits the wall. Run a tape measure from the mark to the floor. Now you know **precisely** how tall you are.

_____ **2.** In this paragraph, the word **precisely** means

    A. partly   **C.** exactly

    B. slightly   **D.** fairly

The rose has long been a sign of **secrecy**. Hundreds of years ago, people wore roses behind their ears. It meant that the people wearing the roses had heard something, but would not tell what they had heard.

_____ **3.** In this paragraph, the word **secrecy** means

    A. riddles   **C.** talking

    B. silence   **D.** sharing

The squid is a sea animal with 10 **tentacles**. It uses eight of them to catch its food. The other two are longer. The squid uses them to bring the food to its mouth.

_____ **4.** In this paragraph, the word **tentacles** means

    A. eyes   **C.** nets

    B. arms   **D.** heads

How can anybody remain underwater for 10 minutes? **Ponder** that question no more. Just fill a glass with water. Then hold it over your head for 10 minutes!

_____ **5.** In this paragraph, the word **ponder** means
- **A.** swim after
- **B.** think about
- **C.** forget about
- **D.** know of

How do pilots avoid **collisions** with other planes in the air? The sky is mapped into highways just like the land is. Signals are sent up from control towers to mark these "skyways." It's a pilot's job to listen to the signals.

_____ **6.** In this paragraph, the word **collisions** means
- **A.** birds
- **B.** crashes
- **C.** insects
- **D.** tires

The trunk of a tree is made up of **annual** rings. Each year a new layer of wood grows to form a new ring. You can tell the age of a tree by counting its rings.

_____ **7.** In this paragraph, the word **annual** means
- **A.** yearly
- **B.** large
- **C.** hard
- **D.** weekly

The Venus flytrap is a plant that **consumes** bugs. When there are no bugs, this plant will gladly accept bits of cheese!

Oh Nooooo!

_____ **8.** In this paragraph, the word **consumes** means
- **A.** eats
- **B.** releases
- **C.** hates
- **D.** grows

In Rome long ago, only the emperor and his family could wear purple. Others were **forbidden** to wear that color!

_____ **1.** In this paragraph, the word **forbidden** means
- **A.** chosen
- **B.** spoken
- **C.** encouraged
- **D.** not allowed

When a whip is snapped, it makes a loud cracking sound. Whips can **accelerate** to a speed of more than 700 miles per hour. At that speed a whip can break the sound barrier.

_____ **2.** In this paragraph, the word **accelerate** means
- **A.** maintain
- **B.** speed up
- **C.** go slower
- **D.** remain the same

Surgeons wore white uniforms until 1914. A doctor thought that the white uniform showed too much blood from **operations**. He wore green instead. Red did not show as much on the green.

_____ **3.** In this paragraph, the word **operations** means
- **A.** surgeries
- **B.** janitors
- **C.** oxygen
- **D.** straps

There is only one flock of whooping cranes in the world. These **endangered** birds live in Canada. They migrate to Texas for the winter. If all the birds in this flock die, the whooping crane will become extinct.

_____ **4.** In this paragraph, the word **endangered** means
- **A.** large
- **B.** white
- **C.** threatened
- **D.** Canadian

The tortoise is the animal that lives the longest. The Mauritius tortoise had a life **span** of 152 years. Some scientists think it lived for 200 years! The Carolina tortoise is found in the United States. Some of these creatures have lived for 123 years.

_____ **5.** In this paragraph, the word **span** means
  A. height   **C.** length
  B. weight   **D.** thirst

What makes popcorn pop? Popcorn kernels are small and hard. There is water within the kernel. When the moisture heats up, it turns to **steam**. The steam causes the kernel to explode.

_____ **6.** In this paragraph, the word **steam** means
  A. dry corn   **C.** melted butter
  B. water vapor   **D.** sea salt

Only one bird can fly **backward**. It is the tiny hummingbird. The bird flies in front of a flower. It sucks the nectar out of the flower. When it is finished, it simply backs up.

_____ **7.** In this paragraph, the word **backward** means
  A. in reverse   **C.** up and down
  B. fast   **D.** like a helicopter

Many people believe that red makes a bull angry and causes him to attack. They believe that is why a bullfighter waves a red cape, but a bull is colorblind. It is the **motion** of the cape that excites the bull. A bullfighter could wave a white or green cape, and the bull would charge.

_____ **8.** In this paragraph, the word **motion** means
  A. color   **C.** stopping
  B. red   **D.** shaking

How can you tell a vegetable from a fruit? In 1893 the Supreme Court passed **judgment** on the subject. If it is consumed with the main course of a meal, it's a vegetable. If it is served as a dessert or snack, it's a fruit.

_____ **1.** In this paragraph, the word **judgment** means

    A. properties   **C.** decision

    B. award   **D.** umpire

Ice cream was first made in China. The explorer Marco Polo described eating dishes of ice **flavored** with fruit. Italians liked it so much they changed the name to Italian ices. The French added cream and renamed it ice cream.

_____ **2.** In this paragraph, the word **flavored** means

    A. given warmth

    B. given taste

    C. given cream

    D. given dishes

Dragonflies are usually seen flying through the air. This happens during the last stage of a dragonfly's life. It can only fly for a few weeks. It spends most of its life under water. Before becoming an **adult**, it lives underwater as a nymph. A nymph looks like a mature dragonfly, but it does not have wings.

_____ **3.** In this paragraph, the word **adult** means

    A. baby   **C.** young

    B. tame   **D.** full-grown

Mistletoe has thick green leaves and white berries. It is never found growing on the ground. This plant does not grow in soil. It grows on the **limbs** of trees.

_____ **4.** In this paragraph, the word **limbs** means

    A. clouds   **C.** roots

    B. branches   **D.** flowers

Ping-Pong is another name for table tennis. Ping-Pong and tennis are very much **alike**. In both games a ball is hit over a net. The name Ping-Pong came from the noise made when the ball was hit by a paddle.

_____ **5.** In this paragraph, the word **alike** means
- **A.** different
- **B.** sounds like
- **C.** hard
- **D.** the same

Dingoes are wild dogs in Australia. No one knows how they got there. The people who moved to the area long ago might have had dogs. Dingoes may be **descendants** of these dogs.

_____ **6.** In this paragraph, the word **descendants** means
- **A.** details
- **B.** offspring
- **C.** parents
- **D.** worlds

The praying mantis is a fierce insect. It **ceases** to move so that it looks like part of a plant. The mantis uses its front legs to trap its prey. It usually catches insects, small frogs, and lizards.

_____ **7.** In this paragraph, the word **ceases** means
- **A.** quits
- **B.** inspects
- **C.** feeds
- **D.** whistles

The giraffe is the tallest animal in the world. It can grow to a height of 20 feet. Giraffes **tower** over people and cars.

_____ **8.** In this paragraph, the word **tower** means
- **A.** run from
- **B.** stand tall
- **C.** knock down
- **D.** work hard

The pygmy marmoset lives in Brazil's forests. It is the smallest monkey. Its head and body are about 6 inches long. You can **barely** feel its fur because its coat is so fine.

_____ **1.** In this paragraph, the word **barely** means
- **A.** coldly
- **B.** hardly
- **C.** lively
- **D.** sweetly

The cone snail has a beautiful marbled shell. Many people like to collect the shell. They must be careful of a living cone snail because it has poisoned **barbs**. The snail's stab is fatal.

_____ **2.** In this paragraph, the word **barbs** means
- **A.** rounded tips
- **B.** golden crowns
- **C.** sharp points
- **D.** dull edges

Libby Riddles wanted to win a famous sled-dog race in Alaska. She knew conditions would be **brutal**, but the blizzards and freezing weather did not stop her. She became the first woman to win the race.

_____ **3.** In this paragraph, the word **brutal** means
- **A.** simple
- **B.** easy
- **C.** ordinary
- **D.** cruel

The Leaning Tower of Pisa is in Italy. The ground on one side of the tower is so soft that the side is **sinking**. This makes the tower lean a tiny bit more each year. People are trying to save it from falling.

_____ **4.** In this paragraph, the word **sinking** means
- **A.** rising higher
- **B.** walking with
- **C.** dropping lower
- **D.** touching against

Dreaming is an important part of sleep. Dreams occur during a period of rapid eye movement. The eyes move quickly during this stage of sleep. If awakened during this period, a person can clearly **recall** the dream.

_____ **5.** In this paragraph, the word **recall** means
    A. remember   **C.** forget
    B. cure   **D.** escape

The zebra belongs to the horse family. It has black and white stripes. The zebra spends time **grazing** on the African plains. Then it goes to watering holes. The lion is its enemy. The zebra bites and kicks to protect itself.

_____ **6.** In this paragraph, the word **grazing** means
    A. drifting in air   **C.** walking by mountains
    B. feeding on grasses   **D.** swimming in streams

A tornado is a very **fierce** storm. This funnel-shaped cloud does not last long. But it sucks up everything in its path. The strong winds can be very destructive.

_____ **7.** In this paragraph, the word **fierce** means
    A. friendly   **C.** dangerous
    B. sticky   **D.** small

The wolf is a large member of the dog family. It is a good hunter. Hoofed animals are its **normal** prey. The wolf inhabits areas that have few people.

_____ **8.** In this paragraph, the word **normal** means
    A. curious   **C.** usual
    B. delicious   **D.** unusual

Writing Roundup

Read each paragraph. Write a word that makes sense on each line.

Aisha was starting to walk home from school

when it began to rain. "Oh, no," she thought.

"I forgot to bring my **(1)** _____ .

Now my **(2)** _____ will get soaked!"

Cody had always wanted to be in the band. He dreamed

of playing a big **(3)** _____ . He was sure that no

one would be able to **(4)** _____ better than he could.

Last spring I tried to build a

birdhouse. I used a hammer and some

(5) _____ . When I finished,

that birdhouse looked **(6)** _____ .

Read each paragraph. Write a sentence that makes sense on each line.

Mrs. Singh was planting

flowers when her spade struck

something hard. She wondered what she should do

next. **(1)** _____. She

gasped in surprise when she saw what the object was.

(2) _____.

Mrs. Singh knew just what she would do with it.

(3) _____.

Carmen needed to earn some money. She really

loved animals. What could she do? **(4)** _____

_____.

Then her next-door neighbor, Ms. Fielder, rang the doorbell.

(5) _____. Now Carmen

has a job, even though it has nothing to do with animals.

(6) _____

_____.

What Is a Main Idea?

The main idea of a paragraph tells what the paragraph is about. The other sentences add details to the main idea. The main idea sentence is often the first or last sentence in the paragraph. But the main idea sentence can be found in the middle of the paragraph too.

The following example may help you think about main ideas:

4   +   6   +   5   =   15

detail + detail + detail = main idea

The numbers *4*, *6*, and *5* are like details. They are smaller than their sum, *15*. The *15*, like a main idea, is bigger. It is made of several smaller parts.

Try It!

Read this story and underline the main idea sentence.

Barbara Jordan is an admired public figure in American history. She was the first African American woman from the South to serve in Congress. She grew up in Texas. Her parents taught her to work hard. Jordan became a lawyer and then entered politics. She tried to make fair laws for everyone.

The main idea sentence is the first sentence in this story about Barbara Jordan. All the other sentences are details.

The main idea could come at the end of the paragraph:

Barbara Jordan was the first African American woman from the South to serve in Congress. She grew up in Texas. Her parents taught her to work hard. She became a lawyer and then entered politics. She tried to make fair laws for everyone. Jordan is an admired public figure in American history.

Practice Finding the Main Idea

This unit asks you to find the main idea of paragraphs.
For instance, read the paragraph and the question below.

You've heard of a full moon and a new moon, but have you heard of a blue moon? Once in a while, there are two full moons in one month. We call the second moon a blue moon. A blue moon appears about every 32 months. So if something happens once in a blue moon, it doesn't happen often.

___C___ **1.** The paragraph mainly tells
      A. why the Moon looks full
      B. how the Moon moves
      C. what a blue moon is
      D. about the different colors of the Moon

The correct answer is **C**. "You've heard of a full moon and a new moon, but have you heard of a blue moon?" is the main idea sentence. The paragraph is about blue moons.

Sometimes a story does not have a main idea sentence. You must read the details in the paragraph. Read the following story. Try to put the details together and find the main idea. Write the letter of your answer in the blank.

When lion cubs are born, they have thick, brown, spotted fur. As many as six cubs are born at one time. The mother lion hides her cubs. She wants to keep them safe from hyenas and leopards. When the cubs are one month old, they meet the lion group.

_____ **2.** The story mainly tells
      A. the number of cubs born at one time
      B. how hyenas and leopards hunt
      C. how much cubs weigh
      D. about the lives of lion cubs

Read each passage. After each passage you will answer a question about the main idea of the passage. Remember, the main idea is the main point in a story.

1. People do not really use music to charm snakes. Snakes have no ears, so they can't hear a flute. The snake charmer startles the snake by waving a hand near it. The snake lifts its head to look around. The charmer then sways back and forth or moves the flute. The snake moves its head to keep an eye on the movement.

_____ **1.** The story mainly tells
    A. why flute music charms snakes
    B. why snakes can't hear sounds
    C. how people really charm snakes
    D. why snakes have no ears

2. A bat can fly at night or even with its eyes closed. If you cover its ears, it can't fly very well. Bats make sounds that people can't hear. The bats find their way by listening to these sounds as they echo off things. Bats even locate insects to eat by following the sounds that bounce off the bugs. People use their eyes, but bats use their ears to know where they're going.

_____ **2.** The story mainly tells
    A. how bats use sound
    B. what things bats often eat as food
    C. how bats fly toward people
    D. how people can hear the sounds of bats

3. Some people say that the White House has ghosts. The most famous ghost is Abraham Lincoln. He is often seen standing in his room looking out the window. Even Eleanor Roosevelt said that she saw him. There is a legend that old Abe walks back and forth all night before something terrible is about to happen.

_____ **3.** The story mainly tells
   A. what Lincoln's ghost is like
   B. when Eleanor Roosevelt's ghost walked
   C. how many ghosts the White House has
   D. how ghosts show when something will happen

---

4. Dolphins are very smart animals. They even have their own language. They talk to each other with clicks, whistles, and grunts. Scientists have been studying this dolphin language. They hope that in the future, people and dolphins will be able to talk to each other.

_____ **4.** The story mainly tells
   A. how dolphins talk to people
   B. how smart dolphins are
   C. how dolphins are different from fish
   D. which scientists are studying languages

5. Deer are the only animals with bones sticking out of their heads. Some animals have horns, but horns aren't bones. They are more like fingernails. Deer have true bones. Every year two new bones grow from the top of a deer's head. At first the bones are soft and covered with skin. Later the skin dries up. The deer rubs off the skin. The bones get hard. The deer uses these horns for fighting.

_____ **5.** The story mainly tells
   A. what deer like to use for fighting
   B. how deer grow bones out of their heads
   C. which animals have horns on their heads
   D. why deer have fingernails

1. Do you believe that air is heavy? If you don't, try this. Put a straw in a glass. Fill the glass with water. Suck on the straw. When you do this, you take all the air out of the straw. The air around the glass pushes down on the water in the glass. It pushes hard. The only place the water can go is up the straw. You can drink through a straw because the weight of the air pushes on the water.

_____ **1.** The story mainly tells
- **A.** how heavy air is
- **B.** how much water to drink
- **C.** how water and air are different
- **D.** how we need air to live

2. For years scientists have wanted to know the spider's secret. The threads of spiderwebs are so tiny, yet so strong. How can these threads be so strong? Now scientists have found out. The inside of the spider's thread is soft. It helps the web stretch without breaking. The outside of the web is hard and strong.

_____ **2.** The story mainly tells
- **A.** who makes thread soft
- **B.** how spiders make strong thread
- **C.** how scientists make strong thread
- **D.** why spiders spin webs

3. Camels have adapted well to the desert. The large humps on their backs hold fat that can serve as food. Camels don't sweat very much, so they don't need much water. The camel's broad feet don't sink in the sand. Long eyelashes and big eyelids protect their eyes from the sun.

_____ **3.** The story mainly tells
- **A.** why camels don't sink in the sand
- **B.** what the hump of a camel is for
- **C.** how the camel is suited to live in the desert
- **D.** why camels do not need a lot of water

4. Bees talk to one another by dancing. When one bee finds flowers for food, it flies back to the hive. The movements it makes tell the bees where the flowers are. If the bee moves in a small circle, the flowers are close. A bee moves slowly in a figure eight when the flowers are more than 100 yards away. Bees may tell about food that is as far as 6 miles away.

_____ **4.** The story mainly tells
     A. how far bees may fly searching for food
     B. how bees talk with each other
     C. what kind of flowering plants bees prefer
     D. how bees collect their food from plants

---

5. Papermakers made the first hot-air balloon. They got the idea when they saw ashes rising from a fire. They turned paper bags upside down over the fire. Just as they had hoped, the bags filled with hot air and floated up. Soon they tried bigger bags made of paper and then cloth. Finally in 1783 people took their first ride in a hot-air balloon. The age of flight had begun!

_____ **5.** The story mainly tells
     A. how the hot-air balloon was invented
     B. how paper bags floated up
     C. why ashes rise over a hot fire
     D. how hot-air balloons are made

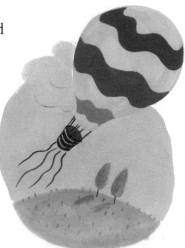

1. People store different kinds of information in different parts of their brains. One area saves only pictures of things we see. Another area remembers how those things are arranged. The area that stores smells and sounds is very close to the area that stores feelings. That's why you sometimes feel happy when you smell homemade bread or sad when you hear a love song.

_____ **1.** The story mainly tells

    A. how we remember pictures

    B. how sounds can affect feelings

    C. when we get different kinds of information

    D. where our brain stores information

2. In 1963 someone made a wide ski to ride down snowy hills. That's how the snowboard was invented. The snowboard looks like a small surfboard. It has sharp edges to cut through snow. To ride it you stand sideways, just as you would on a surfboard. Snowboarding is like surfing on the snow.

_____ **2.** The story mainly tells

    A. how much fun surfing is

    B. how surfing was invented

    C. about the sport of snowboarding

    D. how a surfboard and a skateboard are alike

3. If gum ever sticks on your clothes, don't try to wash it off. Otherwise the gum may never come off. Put an ice cube on the gum. That will harden it so you can try to scrape it off with a table knife. Try nail polish remover. It can sometimes melt gum. If the gum is from a burst bubble, try chewing more gum and using it to lift off the stuck pieces.

_____ **3.** The story mainly tells
- **A.** how chewing gum was invented
- **B.** how to melt gum
- **C.** how to use nail polish remover
- **D.** how to remove gum from your clothes

---

4. The Richter scale measures the strength of an earthquake. An earthquake measuring 2.0 is a weak one. A quake that measures 8.0 is very strong. A quake measuring 1.0 can't be felt. The earthquake that hit San Francisco in 1906 was very strong. It measured about 8.25.

_____ **4.** The story mainly tells
- **A.** what to do during an earthquake
- **B.** about the 1906 San Francisco earthquake
- **C.** about the Richter scale
- **D.** how to measure energy

---

5. Each year a tree grows a layer of new wood just under the bark. When the trunk or a branch is cut, the layers look like rings. Each ring shows one year of growth. To tell how old a tree is, count the rings.

_____ **5.** The story mainly tells
- **A.** how to tell the age of a tree
- **B.** how long a tree lives
- **C.** how to cut a tree
- **D.** how many rings a tree has

1. Birthdays are celebrated in many ways around the world. In Thailand children give gifts to others on their birthdays. A child may give food to a monk. In Mexico a blindfolded child uses a stick to break open a piñata. A piñata is a hollow, paper figure. It is filled with gifts.

_____ **1.** The story mainly tells
    A. about birthday celebrations in different countries
    B. about birthdays in Thailand
    C. about the best way to celebrate a birthday
    D. what a piñata is

2. Twins are born in one out of every 80 births. There are two kinds of twins. The most common twins are fraternal twins. They look no more alike than most other brothers and sisters. One-fourth of all twins born are identical twins. They are the same sex. Identical twins look just alike.

_____ **2.** The story mainly tells
    A. how many twins there are
    B. about two kinds of twins
    C. how fraternal twins look
    D. when identical twins are born

3. Garlic was important in the history of Chicago. Jacques Marquette was a French priest. In 1674 bad health forced him to stop his journey for the winter. He stayed where wild garlic grew. Garlic soup and a fire helped keep Marquette warm. In fact, eating the garlic saved him from getting sick. The place where he stayed was called Checagou. _Checagou_ is a Native American word. It means "place of garlic." That place is now named Chicago.

_____ **3.** The story mainly tells
    A. how Chicago got its name
    B. where Chicago is
    C. how to make garlic soup
    D. about winter in Checagou

4. The gecko, a small lizard, can do something special. It can shed its tail when attacked. When it drops off, the tail wriggles on the ground. The wriggling tail may confuse an attacker. This gives the gecko time to escape. New cells will grow where the tail dropped off. This growth is called a bud. The bud grows into a new tail. After 8 to 12 months, the gecko has a full-sized tail.

_____ **4.** The story mainly tells
    A. what a bud is
    B. how a gecko gets away from its attacker
    C. what a gecko is
    D. about a gecko's unusual tail

---

5. The dandelion is a common weed. It has a bright yellow flower. The leaves are shaped like lions' teeth. Its name comes from three French words, *dent de lion*. Those three words mean "tooth of the lion."

_____ **5.** The story mainly tells
    A. about common weeds
    B. how the dandelion got its name
    C. about dandelion flowers
    D. about lions' teeth

1. The Moon has one-sixth the gravity of Earth. Everything weighs six times less on the Moon. One woman weighs 120 pounds on Earth. On the Moon, the same woman would weigh only 20 pounds. She could jump higher on the Moon than she could on Earth. A blue whale weighs 150 tons. If a blue whale could go to the Moon, it would weigh just 25 tons.

_____ **1.** The story mainly tells
   A. how to get to the Moon
   B. about weight differences on Earth and the Moon
   C. what a woman weighs on the Moon
   D. how much a blue whale weighs

---

2. A crazy quilt is a work of art. People sew together odd-sized pieces of cloth. They don't use any special patterns. They use many different shapes and fabrics. After a backing is attached, the quilt is finished. It looks like a large, beautiful puzzle. Maybe a crazy quilt should have a nicer name.

_____ **2.** The story mainly tells
   A. that a crazy quilt is a work of art
   B. how odd-sized pieces of cloth are used
   C. how a backing is attached
   D. how a crazy quilt looks like a puzzle

3. The world's greatest traveler is the Arctic tern. This bird migrates from one end of Earth to the other. It flies from the Arctic to the Antarctic and back each year. The round trip is about 23,600 miles.

_____ **3.** The story mainly tells
     A. how an Arctic tern looks
     B. about animal movement
     C. about the migration of the Arctic tern
     D. about the Arctic tern's nest

---

4. Forest fires burn thousands of trees each year. They are unsafe to the people and homes in their path. However, fires in forests are not always harmful. Fire is one of nature's ways of destroying problem weeds. Then native plants can return. When thick trees and brush are gone, animals find it easier to get food.

_____ **4.** The story mainly tells
     A. how forest fires start
     B. how forest fires can be helpful
     C. how fires destroy problem weeds
     D. how animals find food

---

5. Sneakers were invented more than 100 years ago. They were called croquet sandals. They cost five times as much as other shoes, so only rich people wore them. Then a company began to make tennis oxfords. Most people could afford these. They were very popular. Soon special sneakers were made for other sports, such as running. Now we have all sorts of sneakers.

_____ **5.** The story mainly tells
     A. how sneakers have changed through the years
     B. which sneakers are right for your sport
     C. what the difference is between shoes and footwear
     D. who could buy croquet sandals

1. The ocean is 7 miles deep in some places, but scuba divers can go down less than a mile. Below that the water pressure is too strong. Scientists have built special submarines that can go deeper. Some of them are made to hold one person. Others can be controlled from ships on the surface. With these subs people go nearly 4 miles down. The deepest parts of the ocean are still a mystery.

_____ **1.** The story mainly tells
   A. how strong the pressure is in the ocean
   B. which submarines can be controlled from ships
   C. how water pressure affects exploring in the ocean
   D. how people see the bottom of the ocean

---

2. Thousands of years ago, someone was traveling across the desert. For food he carried sheep's milk in a goatskin bag. The hot desert sun turned the milk thick and sour. He was hungry, so he ate the strange stuff. To his surprise he liked it! That's how yogurt was discovered.

_____ **2.** The story mainly tells
   A. which foods to take in the desert
   B. how yogurt tastes
   C. how yogurt was first made
   D. how to stay alive in the desert

---

3. Many green leaves, which are food factories for trees, change color in the fall. Their green coloring makes food out of sunlight, air, and water. When the days grow shorter in the fall, these factories slow down and then finally stop. The green slowly fades away. Where do the yellow, orange, and brown come from? They were in the leaves all the time, but the green was too bright for the other colors to show.

_____ **3.** The story mainly tells
   A. why leaves change color in the fall
   B. how leaves make food from sunlight, air, and water
   C. what the parts of a tree are
   D. what food factories make

4. When baseball was new, players had to throw the ball and hit the runner to make an out. The ball had to be big and soft so the runners wouldn't be hurt. Later, players used the tag as a way to make an out. This made the game more exciting, and it caused some other big changes. The ball could be smaller and harder. The smaller ball could be thrown faster, and batters could hit it farther. Thus the modern game of baseball was born.

_____ **4.** The story mainly tells
A. how baseball changed
B. how people used to make an out in baseball
C. how large old baseballs were
D. how far a modern baseball can be hit

---

5. If you are going on a picnic, don't wear anything that smells good. Some insects are crazy about perfume. Bees will smell you and come swarming. People have also found that bees like bright, flowery material. It seems that some insects just can't tell the difference between the real thing and a copy!

_____ **5.** The story mainly tells
A. when to wear perfume
B. how to dress well on trips
C. how to avoid bees on picnics
D. how some things can attract insects

1. It takes practice and skill to throw a Frisbee. Be sure your index finger is lined up on the outside rim. Tilt the edge of the Frisbee that is opposite your thumb downward. The stronger the wind, the more the Frisbee should be tilted. You need a strong wrist. It's the snap of your wrist that sends your Frisbee spinning.

_____ **1.** The story mainly tells
- **A.** how to throw a Frisbee
- **B.** how important strong wrists are
- **C.** what to do in a strong wind
- **D.** how to aim at your target

---

2. Why do rabbits always seem as if they have itchy noses? Experts say the nose wiggling helps keep their nose tissue damp. This improves their sense of smell. Rabbits adjust their air intake in this way, too. It keeps them cool on hot days. Sometimes nose wiggling simply means rabbits are excited.

_____ **2.** The story mainly tells
- **A.** why rabbits wiggle their noses
- **B.** how a rabbit improves its sense of smell
- **C.** why rabbits adjust their air intake
- **D.** what rabbits do when they are excited

3. Maybe you have seen flamingos in a zoo. These brightly colored birds with long necks look too pink to be real. Wild flamingos get their bright-pink feathers from the plants and fish they eat. However, in zoos they don't eat the same things they do in the wild. They could turn white. To keep this from happening, the zookeepers give these birds a special pill.

_____ **3.** The story mainly tells
- **A.** how flamingos stay pink
- **B.** what flamingos eat
- **C.** what kinds of birds there are
- **D.** how birds in zoos get pink

---

4. If you sneeze, you'll almost always hear someone say "bless you." Some historians think that people started saying "bless you" more than 1,000 years ago in Europe. At that time the plague was spreading everywhere. One of the first signs of this terrible sickness was sneezing. People thought the blessing might help keep them from getting sick.

_____ **4.** The story mainly tells
- **A.** how a disease spread across Europe
- **B.** what happens to the body when people sneeze
- **C.** how the saying "bless you" got started
- **D.** why sneezing is a sign of getting sick

---

5. Scientists are studying a sea turtle. She lives in a tank in Boston. The scientists think she can teach them how she uses hearing to sense her world. She is being trained to respond to signals.

_____ **5.** The story mainly tells
- **A.** about turtle senses
- **B.** where the turtle lives
- **C.** how turtles make signals
- **D.** what scientists hope to learn from the turtle

1. Television was invented in the 1920s. Few people had televisions until the 1950s. Forty years later, 98 percent of the households in the United States had a television. Watching television is a popular activity. Many homes have two or more televisions. Americans watch more than 1,500 hours of television per person each year.

_____ **1.** The story mainly tells
    A. the history of television commercials
    B. when television was invented
    C. what television-watching habits Americans have
    D. how televisions actually work

---

2. When their enemies chase them, ostriches lie down on the sand. The giant birds stretch their necks out flat on the ground. When they lie there, the loose feathers on their bodies look like bushes. Ostriches don't need to hide often. Their strong legs are good for both running and fighting.

_____ **2.** The story mainly tells
    A. how ostriches stick their heads in the sand
    B. how smart ostriches are
    C. how ostriches avoid their enemies
    D. how strong ostrich legs are

---

3. Ballet dancers often spin around and around. Why don't they become dizzy? A dancer's body turns smoothly. The dancer holds his or her head still and then jerks it around quickly. This way the head is still most of the time. The dancer does not become dizzy.

_____ **3.** The story mainly tells
    A. why a dancer spins
    B. how to become a ballet dancer
    C. where a ballet dancer practices
    D. why a dancer does not become dizzy when doing turns

4. An octopus gets its name from its eight arms. There have been new discoveries about these sea creatures. Experts have found that an octopus has a memory. It uses that memory to solve problems. An octopus in danger uses a built-in defense. It squirts a stream of ink to help it hide.

_____ **4.** The story mainly tells
   A. that an octopus has eight arms
   B. how an octopus uses its memory
   C. some interesting facts about octopuses
   D. how an octopus can squirt a stream of ink

---

5. It is important to put a return address on mail. Mail with a wrong mailing address goes to the dead-letter office. There postal workers open it to search for clues. If they don't find any, the mail is thrown away. The post office can sell items of value. It keeps the money.

_____ **5.** The story mainly tells
   A. how to write a letter
   B. what can happen to mail with no return address
   C. how mail gets thrown away
   D. how the post office makes money

Writing Roundup

Read each paragraph. Think about the main idea. Write the main idea in your own words.

1. A few rabbits were the start of a big problem in Australia. They were set free. Ten years later there were millions of rabbits. They were all over the country. They were eating farm crops. It took a while to find ways to control them.

What is the main idea of this paragraph?

_____

_____

2. Tom Bradley was the first African American to become a lieutenant on the Los Angeles police force. He was also the first African American on the city council. He was the first African American mayor in the city. The people of Los Angeles loved him. They kept him as mayor for almost 20 years.

What is the main idea of this paragraph?

_____

_____

3. Iron Eyes Cody was a Native American actor. In 1971, a tear changed his life. He shed the tear in a TV ad about keeping America clean. The ad became very popular, and Iron Eyes became famous for his tear. He was remembered for it even after his death in 1999.

What is the main idea of this paragraph?

_____

_____

Prewriting

Think of a main idea that you would like to write about, such as an interesting country, what you would do if you were mayor of your city, or what it would be like to be in a TV ad. Fill in the chart below.

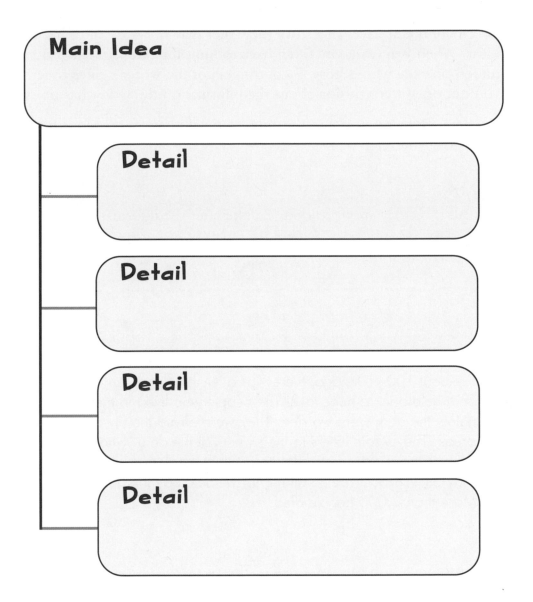

Main Idea

Detail

Detail

Detail

Detail

On Your Own

Now use another sheet of paper to write your paragraph. Underline the sentence that tells the main idea.

What Is a Conclusion?

A conclusion is a decision you make after thinking about all the information you have. In a story the writer may not state all of his or her ideas. When you read, you often have to hunt for clues so that you can understand the whole story. By putting all of the writer's clues together, you can draw a conclusion about the information the writer has not stated.

There are many stories in this unit. You will draw conclusions based on each story you read.

Try It!

Read this story about a flood. Think about the information it gives you.

About 100 years ago, there was a terrible flood. An old, dirt dam held back a huge lake. The people who lived in the valley below the dam were worried. They were afraid the dam would break. They wrote letters to the owners of the dam, who lived far away. One owner wrote back to say that the dam was safe. On May 31, 1889, it rained all night. The next day the dam broke. More than 2,000 people died.

What conclusion can you draw? Write your conclusion on the lines.

_____

_____

You might have written something such as, "The people who lived in the valley knew that the dam was not safe," or "The owners weren't worried about the dam." You can draw these conclusions from the paragraph. The second sentence says that the dam was old and built of dirt. This made the valley people worry that the dam would break. They were worried enough to write letters to the owners, but the owners did nothing to make the dam stronger. The sixth sentence tells us that one owner replied that the dam was safe. From these clues, you can draw the above conclusions.

Using What You Know

Read the stories on this page. Hunt for clues that will tell you the time of year for each.

It's getting too cold to wear shorts and sandals. Now I need warm clothes when I go outside. The colors of the leaves on most of the trees are changing. Instead of green, they are now all shades of red, orange, and brown. I like to collect the beautiful, dried-out leaves.

It is _____.

My mother and aunt have been cooking all day long. My sister and I have been watching a football game on television. It's almost time to eat. Turkey and dressing, vegetables, cranberry sauce, and a pumpkin pie are on the table. When we sit down, we will think about the things for which we are thankful.

It is _____.

Even though it's been a very hot day in the middle of summer, we've had a good time. This morning we watched a parade and listened to a speech. Then we went on a picnic with some friends. We ate hamburgers and watermelon. Tonight we will go down to the river and watch the fireworks. They are supposed to be even better than last year's.

It is _____.

I've been cutting out red paper hearts all day. I'm going to paste them on sheets of white paper that I've folded in half to make cards. Then I'll write a saying inside of each card. I'll also make a small hole on the folded edge of each card so that I can tie some red and pink ribbons. Tomorrow I'll give each of my friends one of my special cards, along with some candy hearts.

It is _____.

Read each passage. After each passage you will answer a question that will require you to draw a conclusion about the story. Remember, a conclusion is a decision you make after putting together all the clues you are given.

1. Serious dancers begin their training when they're very young. By the age of three, these dancers have already begun to learn a few dance steps. Dancers spend years learning how to move smoothly. They practice for hours each day. Still, young dancers must go to school like other children. The only time they can practice dance is after school.

_____ 1. From this story you can tell that
   A. most dancers never learn spelling
   B. learning how to dance is a secret
   C. dancers have to work very hard
   D. three-year-olds are the best dancers

2. Have you ever tugged on a chicken's wishbone? You might know the custom. The one who wins the larger piece gets to make a wish. Did you know this custom is more than 2,000 years old? The Etruscan people first practiced the custom. They thought that chickens could read the future. They believed a hen could predict the laying of an egg with her squawk. They also thought a rooster could predict the dawn with his crow.

_____ 2. From this story you can tell that
   A. some beliefs are very old
   B. the Etruscan people liked to eat chicken
   C. wishbones have magical powers
   D. the loser in a wishbone tug will have bad luck

3. Ramesh and Maya were happy. In seven months they would have a child. Maya ate good food and exercised. She saw the doctor each month. Ramesh helped fix a room for the child. Together they read books on raising children.

_____ **3.** From this story you can tell that
  A. they wanted to take good care of their child
  B. the baby would be born in July
  C. Ramesh was good at fixing things
  D. Maya loved to cook

4. Dr. Pavlov did scientific tests on dogs. He noticed that hungry dogs drooled when they saw food, so he rang a bell before he fed them. He did this over and over again. After several days he rang the bell, but he didn't feed the dogs then. The hungry dogs still drooled when they heard the bell, even though there wasn't any food. Pavlov found one way that animals learn things.

_____ **4.** From this story you can tell that
  A. a ringing bell always makes animals hungry
  B. the dogs expected food when they heard the bell
  C. Pavlov probably lived a long, long time ago
  D. Pavlov loved dogs

5. Computers read signals that travel along wires. These signals move very fast. They move as fast as light. Signals that travel on very long wires sometimes get mixed up. When this happens, the computers don't work anymore. New computers use shorter wires. This keeps them from having so many problems.

_____ **5.** From this story you can tell that
  A. computers can read better than people
  B. computers move faster than light
  C. the length of computer wires is important
  D. computer problems can't be fixed

1. Spaceships can go 7 miles per second. That sounds fast, but it's really slow. A trip to Mars takes a spaceship about nine months. Light is much faster. It travels about 200,000 miles per second. Light travels faster than anything else. If people could ride on a ray of light, a trip to Mars would take five minutes.

_____ **1.** From this story you can tell that
     A. spaceships can now move as fast as light
     B. long space trips will need very fast spaceships
     C. a trip around Earth would take five minutes
     D. traveling in space is dangerous

2. People used to ride a bike called the ordinary. The back wheel was about 1 foot high. The front wheel was about 5 feet high. When this tall bike hit a little bump, the bike often fell over. Later people began riding the safety bike. Its two wheels were about the same size.

_____ **2.** From this story you can tell that the safety bike
     A. was probably longer than the ordinary
     B. was most likely made of iron
     C. was probably not as dangerous as the ordinary
     D. was invented 100 years ago

3. There weren't always oranges in Europe. People from the Far East brought oranges to Europe during the Middle Ages. Later, sailors from Europe brought oranges to America. Now the United States grows a million tons of oranges each year.

_____ **3.** From this story you can tell that
     A. the first oranges probably grew in the Far East
     B. orange trees make fruit only in winter
     C. orange trees have blue flowers
     D. there were many wars during the Middle Ages

4. Once dodo birds lived on an island. They ate the seeds of one kind of tree. The seeds had hard shells. Dodo birds had strong stomachs. Their stomach juices broke up the shells. Because of this, the seeds could grow. The last dodo birds died out years ago. Scientists found that the trees were dying out, too. They wanted to save the trees, so they decided to feed the hard seeds to turkeys. Turkeys have strong stomachs. With their help the trees live on.

_____ **4.** From this story you can tell that
  A. animals ate all the dodo birds years ago
  B. the seeds were the dodo's only food
  C. the tree couldn't grow without a bird's help
  D. birds can't eat seeds with hard shells

---

5. Tugboats help link the city of Seattle to the sea. The small, strong tugs guide large ships into and out of the harbor. Without the tugs the big ships could not make the trip safely. To honor the tugs, Seattle holds tugboat races each spring. At that time the harbor is full of stubby boats splashing in the water like playful whales

_____ **5.** You can tell that tugs are
  A. used only in the spring
  B. unsafe
  C. hard to steer
  D. necessary

1. When it is hot in India, people have a tasty way to stay cool. They eat mangoes. The mango is a fruit. It looks something like an apple. On the inside the mango is soft and yellow. In India the mango gives relief even when the temperature is higher than 100 degrees.

_____ **1.** You can tell that
    A. mangoes grow in cool climates
    B. mangoes probably sell well in India when it's hot
    C. Indians like apples
    D. mangoes make good jams

2. Many American children love peanut butter. Many adults like it too. Peanut butter is served for lunch in many schools. Some people like it for a snack, and others have it at breakfast.

_____ **2.** From the story you can tell that peanut butter
    A. sticks to the roof of your mouth
    B. is popular with all ages
    C. is always crunchy
    D. is best as a lunch food

3. In Hawaii people make pretty necklaces called leis. A lei is made of flowers. A single lei often has more than 400 blossoms. The blossoms are attached by the stems. Leis are worn at special events. Important visitors are also given leis to show that they are welcome.

_____ **3.** To make a lei, you would need
- **A.** to grow flowers
- **B.** to be an important person
- **C.** to have many flowers
- **D.** an invitation to a party

---

4. Today a book is a stack of printed papers bound in a cover. Today's books are easy to carry, but years ago books were different. Each book was made of heavy clay tablets with carvings on them. The tablets of one book filled a long shelf. It would have taken many trips to carry such a book from the shelf to a reading table.

_____ **4.** One clay tablet can best be compared to
- **A.** a page in a modern book
- **B.** a carving in a museum
- **C.** the cover of a book
- **D.** part of a library shelf

---

5. Military ants may be small, but people and animals run when they see them. Thousands of these ants travel together through the thick jungles of South America. The ants swarm over any animal in their path. They can eat birds, animals, snakes, and even humans. The ants are always on the move, and they are always hungry.

_____ **5.** Military ants are dangerous mainly because they
- **A.** live in the jungle
- **B.** are always on the move
- **C.** are so small
- **D.** eat any living thing in their path

1. Clownfish are small, colorful saltwater fish. They are bright orange with black and white stripes. These fish are found in the warm waters of the Pacific Ocean near coral reefs. They live among sea anemones, which protect them.

_____ **1.** This story does <u>not</u> tell
   A. the colors on the body of a clownfish
   B. where clownfish live
   C. how the sea anemones protect the clownfish
   D. what kind of water the clownfish needs

---

2. May 6 is a special day for the people of Northville, New York. Every year on that day, a flock of swifts returns to the town. The birds fly to Northville from their winter home in Peru. They circle over a large chimney in a vacant factory. Then they settle into the chimney as the people watch.

_____ **2.** After the swifts arrive, they probably
   A. look for smoke
   B. go back to Peru
   C. build nests
   D. build fires

---

3. Ranchers in Texas had a problem. Coyotes and other wild animals were killing their sheep and goats, so some ranchers began using donkeys to protect the herds. The donkeys do a good job. The coyotes are terrified of the teeth and sharp hooves of the donkeys.

_____ **3.** You can tell that when donkeys see coyotes they
   A. kick and bite
   B. tell the ranchers
   C. run away
   D. hide the herds

4. What drink do we like on a hot day? Lots of people drink lemonade. This sweet and sour drink cools us off. Children set up stands to sell it. Families take it on picnics. Neighbors sip it on porches. Lemonade is popular in America. It was first made in Paris, France, in 1630.

_____ **4.** From the story you can tell that
  A. most lemonade comes from Paris, France
  B. more lemonade is sold in summer than in winter
  C. lemonade is heated before it is served
  D. lemonade is a healthy drink

5. The man wriggled his toes in the sand and then returned to the towel on the ground. He picked up the pair of binoculars by the towel and looked through them. The ship in the distance didn't have an American flag. But he couldn't tell what country's flag the ship was flying.

_____ **5.** You can tell that the man
  A. is a spy for a foreign country
  B. is standing on a beach looking out in the ocean
  C. doesn't have very much money
  D. is camping in the mountains during the winter

1. Many Americans like to eat Chinese food. At the end of the meal, fortune cookies are served. These folded-up cookies have messages in them. Some messages tell what the future will bring. Other messages give advice. Still others are just wise sayings. All messages are written for Americans. Fortune cookies are never served in China.

_____ 1. From this story you can tell that
    A. the messages are in Chinese
    B. people in China can't read
    C. fortune cookies are an American custom
    D. people in China don't like cookies

2. Weddings have many customs. Cakes are a special part of these customs. Wedding cakes were not always eaten as they are today. Long ago, guests threw small wheat cakes at the bride. Wheat was considered a sign of good fortune. By throwing cakes, guests wished the bride a happy marriage. Later, in the Middle Ages, guests began the custom of eating wedding cakes.

_____ **2.** From this story you can tell that
    A. early people did not like to eat cakes
    B. some wedding customs have changed
    C. early people liked to waste food
    D. people today should throw cakes at brides

3. What causes the traffic light to change colors? A timer in a box near the light is set for a certain number of seconds. The number of seconds isn't the same all the time. At night when there's less traffic, the light may change more slowly.

_____ **3.** You can tell that during rush hour
  A. the light stays red all the time
  B. the lights change more quickly
  C. the timer always breaks
  D. the light stays yellow

_____

4. These days we find zippers on many products, but there was no such thing as a zipper available before 1893. That was the year Whitcomb Judson designed the zipper. His device often jammed. Twenty years later Gideon Sundback improved the zipper. It was not popular on clothes for another ten years. B. F. Goodrich named it *zipper* because of the sound it made when pulled.

_____ **4.** The story suggests that the zipper
  A. improved by Sundback didn't jam
  B. was an immediate success
  C. was used on clothes before 1893
  D. was invented by B. F. Zipper

_____

5. Farmers have known for a long time that pigs like toys. Research shows that when pigs play with toys, they are less likely to harm one another. What kind of toys do pigs like? Reports say that pigs are fond of rubber hoses. They like to shake them and chew on the ends.

_____ **5.** You can tell that
  A. toys help improve the way pigs behave
  B. pigs like to play with balls
  C. farmers play with pigs
  D. pigs do not share their toys

1. Hockey is one of the oldest games in the world. The ancient Greeks and Persians played it. So did Native Americans. The name comes from an old French word, *hoquet*. It is the word for a shepherd's crooked stick, or staff.

_____ **1.** From this story you can tell that
    A. hockey is played with a ball
    B. the French have played hockey for a long time
    C. hockey is now played by shepherds
    D. hockey will not last much longer

2. Millie frowned as she looked up at the sky. She pulled up the neck of her jacket and hunched down inside it. Despite the heavy air, the wind was rough. As Millie crossed the street, the first drops began to fall. She quickened her pace in the darkening day.

_____ **2.** In this story the weather is
    A. snowy
    B. stormy
    C. sunny
    D. warm

3. He heard the steady drumming sound he made on the pavement. One foot was becoming sore, but he didn't let himself feel the pain. At last he passed the park bench with the broken seat. "One more mile to go," he thought.

_____ **3.** From this you can tell that the man
    A. is running in a gym
    B. is running along a route he often takes
    C. is a stranger to the neighborhood
    D. has broken his foot

4. Miniature horses are becoming very popular. A miniature horse looks like a horse but is only as big as a German shepherd dog. These little horses come in many colors. They can learn tricks and earn ribbons at horse shows. Best of all, they eat much less than regular horses do.

_____ **4.** You can tell that the little horses
  A. can pull big loads
  B. are fast compared to normal horses
  C. can only be brown
  D. cannot be ridden by an adult

---

5. A steeplechase is a horse race. The path of the race goes through ditches and over hedges. It might also go across streams. The name for this race comes from England. In the 1700s, riders would get together for a race in the country. They would pick out a distant church steeple and race to it.

_____ **5.** From this story you <u>cannot</u> tell if
  A. the riders were English
  B. the riders were in the country
  C. the riders were on horses
  D. the riders were men or women

1. Bob Siekman of Pyote, Texas, has an unusual hobby. He collects old fire trucks. As a youth, Bob watched a man build a fire truck. Young Bob thought fires and fire trucks were very exciting. As a man, Bob continued his interest in fire trucks by collecting them. He has five old fire trucks in his collection.

_____ **1.** The story does <u>not</u> tell
   A. where Bob Siekman lives
   B. about Siekman's hobby
   C. how many old fire trucks Siekman owns
   D. where Siekman finds the old fire trucks

2. Do you know about the Seven Wonders of the Ancient World? These structures were built long, long ago. One was the Lighthouse at Pharos in Egypt. It stood more than 400 feet tall. Another was the Colossus of Rhodes on an island near Turkey. This bronze statue was almost 200 feet tall. All but one of these wonders have disappeared. You can still see the Great Pyramids in Egypt.

_____ **2.** The story suggests that
   A. the Colossus was in Egypt
   B. six of the ancient wonders no longer exist
   C. the Great Pyramids have disappeared
   D. the Colossus was taller than the Lighthouse

3. Alfred Wegener looked at a world map. He noticed a strange thing. All the continents looked like jigsaw pieces. All the pieces seemed to fit together. Wegener thought about this idea for a long time. In 1912, he offered a new theory. He claimed that all the continents were once a large landmass. Then over time the continents moved apart. Wegener called his theory "continental drift." Other scientists did not accept his ideas until 40 years later.

_____ **3.** The story suggests that Wegener's theory
   A. was about jigsaw puzzles
   B. was accepted immediately
   C. did not have a name
   D. explained how the continents were formed

4. You have probably seen a lightning flash, but often you don't hear the sound of thunder until a few seconds later. You can use a simple formula to learn how far from you the lightning struck. When you see the flash of lightning, start counting seconds. When you hear the thunder, stop counting. Sound travels at 1,200 feet per second. Multiply 1,200 by the number of seconds you counted. Then you will know how many feet from you the lightning flashed.

_____ **4.** You can tell from the story that
    A. light travels at 1,200 feet per second
    B. sound travels faster than light
    C. thunder always comes before lightning
    D. light travels faster than sound

5. Trees are very useful plants. They help provide us with air to breathe. Trees take in carbon dioxide and give off oxygen. This action is known as photosynthesis, but this action works only with sunlight. At night the process is reversed.

_____ **5.** This story suggests that trees
    A. grow very tall
    B. like kids climbing in them
    C. give off carbon dioxide at night
    D. sleep at night

1. Have you ever tied a string on your finger? The purpose of the string is to help you remember something. This practice comes from an old European superstition. People once thought that they could trap a wish until it came true. To trap the wish, they would tie a string on one finger. They thought that the string would keep the wish from leaving the body.

_____ **1.** The story does <u>not</u> tell
  A. why people today tie a string on one finger
  B. why people used to tie a string on one finger
  C. where this practice began
  D. on which finger you should tie the string

2. If you look under your kitchen sink, you will see some drain pipes. One pipe is U-shaped. It is called a trap. Harmful gases develop in a sewer line. The curved part of the trap holds a small amount of water. The water closes off the pipe. The trap keeps you safe. The gases can't enter your house and harm you.

_____ **2.** The story suggests that the trap
  A. is a straight pipe
  B. lets harmful gases enter your house
  C. is not part of the drain pipe
  D. has a very useful purpose

3. José was taking guitar lessons. He wanted to join a band when he got older. José's lessons were on Fridays after school. His teacher thought José was a fast learner. She gave him harder and harder things to play. José could play them all.

_____ **3.** This story does <u>not</u> tell
  A. what José wants to do when he gets older
  B. when José goes to his guitar lessons
  C. what kind of music José likes to play
  D. what José's teacher thinks of his ability

4. In 1901, Jagadis Bose talked to the Royal Society in London. Bose thought that plants had senses just like people. As Bose spoke, the scientists there laughed at him. Bose was not discouraged. He returned to his home in India. He began tests to prove his claims. After years of work, Bose had his proof. His tests showed that plants have all the senses except hearing. When Bose returned to the Royal Society, he was cheered. The scientists there soon made him a member.

_____ **4.** The story does <u>not</u> tell
   A. where the Royal Society is located
   B. where Jagadis Bose lived
   C. what kinds of plants Bose tested
   D. what Bose's tests proved

---

5. Are you familiar with the belief about broken mirrors? If you break one, you are supposed to have seven years of bad luck or ill health. This belief is about 2,000 years old. The early Romans were the first to have this notion. They thought that a person's health changed in cycles of seven years. They believed that mirrors reflected one's health. So to break a mirror was to break one's health.

_____ **5.** The story does <u>not</u> tell
   A. what is supposed to happen if you break a mirror
   B. how old this notion is
   C. what the Romans thought about the cycles of health
   D. what might happen if you fix a broken mirror

Writing Roundup

Read each paragraph. Think about a conclusion you can draw. Write your conclusion in a complete sentence.

1. Jim Thorpe was a Native American. He won fame in track and field in the Olympic Games. He also won fame as a star player in the early days of football. Thorpe had other skills, too. For six years he played major-league baseball. In one of those years, he batted right-handed and left-handed!

What conclusion can you draw from this paragraph?

_____

_____

2. Until 1952, two titles of respect were used before a woman's name. One was *Miss*. This title meant the woman was single. Another was *Mrs.* This title showed that the woman was married. In 1952, another title was added. It was *Ms.* This meant the person was a woman. She might be either single or married.

What conclusion can you draw from this paragraph?

_____

_____

3. The year 2004 marked the twentieth year of the show of a famous TV talk show host. Her name is Oprah Winfrey. When she started, her show was seen only in the Chicago area. It wasn't long before TV stations all over wanted Oprah. Two years later her show was on everywhere. She soon had the most popular talk show on television.

What conclusion can you draw from this paragraph?

_____

_____

Read the paragraph below. What conclusion can you draw? Use the clues in the paragraph to answer the questions in complete sentences.

Paco was glad his grandfather had come to visit. He was glad to share his room with his mother's father. His grandfather told Paco stories about their family. They had come from Mexico. They moved to Texas in 1847. That was only two years after Texas became a state. They may still have some family in Mexico. Paco's grandfather did not know. "It seems like we've always been in Texas," he told Paco. "My father was born here. His father was born here, too."

1. Does Paco's grandfather live with Paco? How do you know?

_____

_____

2. Did Paco have the same last name as his grandfather? How do you know?

_____

_____

3. When did Texas become a state? How do you know?

_____

_____

4. Does Paco's grandfather seem interested in finding more family in Mexico? How do you know?

_____

_____

What Is an Inference?

An inference is a guess you make after thinking about what you already know. Suppose you are going to see a movie. From what you know about movies, you might infer that you will wait in line to buy a ticket. You will watch the movie on a large screen in a dark theater.

An author does not write every detail in a story. If every detail were told, stories would be long and boring, and the main point would be lost. Suppose you read, "Jane rode her bike to the park." The writer does not have to tell you what a park is. You already know that it is a place where people go to have fun outdoors. From what you know, you might guess that people who go to a park can play ball, swim, or play on the swings. By filling in these missing details, you could infer that Jane went to the park to meet friends for a ball game. You can infer the missing details from what you know.

Try It!

Read this story about Harriet Beecher Stowe. Think about the facts.

Harriet Beecher Stowe lived in the 1800s. At that time some people owned slaves. Stowe knew that slavery was wrong and wanted to speak out against it. She wrote a book called *Uncle Tom's Cabin.* It was published in 1852. It was the story of Tom, a good man who was a slave. It told about how badly slaves were treated. This book made many people think about slavery.

What inference can you make about Harriet Beecher Stowe? Write an inference on the line below.

_____

You might have written something such as, "Stowe hoped to help slaves by writing a book about how bad slavery was." You can make this inference by putting together the facts in the story and what you already know. You know that people who have strong feelings about something want to help.

Practice Making Inferences

Read each story. Then read the statements after each story. Some are facts. They can be found in the story. Other statements are inferences. Decide whether each statement is a fact or an inference. The first one has been done for you.

Tim and John played basketball together each day after school. One day Tim started shouting that John was not playing fair. John took his basketball and went home. The next day John didn't show up at the basketball court.

Fact	Inference		
○	●	**1.** **A.**	Tim and John were friends.
●	○	**B.**	Tim and John played basketball together.
●	○	**C.**	John took his basketball and went home.
○	●	**D.**	John was angry with Tim the next day.

You can find statements **B** and **C** in the story, so they are facts. You can infer that the boys were friends, but that isn't stated in the story, so statement **A** is an inference. We don't know for sure why John didn't come to the basketball court, so statement **D** is also an inference.

Alfred Nobel was a Swedish inventor. He invented dynamite in 1867. Nobel was worried about how dynamite would be used. He hoped it would be used for peaceful purposes. He established a fund that gave awards each year. These awards are called Nobel Prizes. They are given for works of writing and of science. They are also given to those who have done special things for peace.

Fact	Inference		
○	○	**2.** **A.**	Nobel was an inventor.
○	○	**B.**	Nobel was a strong supporter of world peace.
○	○	**C.**	Nobel believed that war was bad.
○	○	**D.**	Some Nobel prizes are given for writing.

Read the passages. Use what you know about inference to answer the questions. Remember, an inference is a guess you make by putting together what you know and what you read or see in the stories.

1. Pam and Pat tried out for the soccer team. The coach needed only one more player. She needed a good goalie to block the other team's shots. Last year the team lost every game by more than five goals. During tryouts Pam passed the ball well but couldn't block goal shots. As a practice goalie, Pat saved many shots.

Fact	Inference		
○	○	**1.** **A.**	The coach picked Pat to be on the team.
○	○	**B.**	A good goalie can help a team win.
○	○	**C.**	Pat and Pam tried out for the soccer team.
○	○	**D.**	Pam could pass the ball well.

2. It was spring and time to get the garden ready for planting. Chris had a load of dirt delivered to his backyard. For two whole days, Chris shoveled dirt into a wheelbarrow. He put the dirt in the garden. He went back and forth between the dirt pile and the garden. It took many hours and much hard work. On the third day, he saw his neighbor coming over with a wheelbarrow.

Fact	Inference		
○	○	**2.** **A.**	Chris needed another wheelbarrow.
○	○	**B.**	Chris hoped his neighbor would help.
○	○	**C.**	Chris put the dirt in the garden.
○	○	**D.**	Chris had the dirt delivered.

3. One rainy day Nan noticed water dripping from the ceiling. That was when she knew she needed a new roof. She asked a few people for their advice. One person told her that putting new shingles over the old roof would make it too heavy. Another person told her that it would be all right to add another layer of shingles.

Fact	Inference		
○	○	**3. A.**	Nan needs a new roof.
○	○	**B.**	Two people gave Nan different advice.
○	○	**C.**	A heavy roof might fall into the house.
○	○	**D.**	Nan can't do the job by herself.

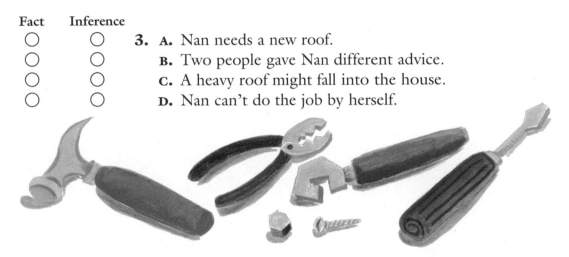

4. Maria's mother gave her a tool kit. It has tools in the lid and in the bottom. The tools fit into molded plastic trays with a place shaped like each tool. On the top are wrenches and sockets. The sockets are both English and metric sizes. In the bottom tray are screwdrivers, pliers, and a ratchet. Maria is excited about using the tools.

Fact	Inference		
○	○	**4. A.**	Maria's mother knows what Maria likes.
○	○	**B.**	The tool kit has screwdrivers.
○	○	**C.**	All the tools fit into one box.
○	○	**D.**	Sockets can come in different sizes.

5. Don had a beautiful lawn. It looked like a thick, green carpet. Don's next-door neighbor Fred's lawn looked awful. It had weeds and patches of brown grass, and there were some places where grass didn't grow at all. Both Don and Fred watered their lawns. They also cut the grass once a week. Don always put fertilizer on his lawn in the fall and spring, but Fred did not.

Fact	Inference		
○	○	**5. A.**	Don and Fred watered their lawns.
○	○	**B.**	Don and Fred cut their lawns once a week.
○	○	**C.**	Don took good care of his lawn.
○	○	**D.**	Grass needs fertilizer to stay green.

1. Frank loved to play tennis, and he was on the tennis court every day. Frank could hit the ball very hard. He was a good player. One day he met his friend Jim for a game of tennis. Jim had just started playing tennis. After the game Frank said, "I will help you with your shots, Jim."

Fact	Inference		
○	○	**1.** **A.**	Frank loved to play tennis.
○	○	**B.**	Frank and Jim met for a game of tennis.
○	○	**C.**	Frank won the game.
○	○	**D.**	Jim was not a good tennis player.

2. Chicago is one of the few places where people play softball with a 16-inch ball. Most softballs are smaller. The rules for softball are like the rules for baseball, but most of the players don't use gloves or mitts. The pitcher throws the ball underhand. It is hard to hit a softball a long distance.

Fact	Inference		
○	○	**2.** **A.**	People in Chicago like the 16-inch ball.
○	○	**B.**	Most softball players don't use mitts.
○	○	**C.**	Baseball players need mitts.
○	○	**D.**	Most softballs are smaller than 16 inches.

3. Many young people are interested in the past. They can learn facts about the past from their families. Grandparents can give many facts. Rachel likes to record her grandfather's stories about growing up on a farm in the early 1900s. Rachel shares the stories with her friends. They are always surprised at how people lived during that time. "How could they live without air-conditioning?" one friend asked.

Fact	Inference		
○	○	**3.** **A.**	Families pass on their past experiences.
○	○	**B.**	Grandparents know about the past.
○	○	**C.**	Children are interested in the past.
○	○	**D.**	Many things have changed over the years

4. When you recycle something, you use it again. Paper and glass can be recycled. Some cities help people recycle. People put used paper, plastic, glass, and cans into bins. The city makes sure that these objects aren't just thrown away but are made into new items. Years ago these things were buried, but they took up too much space.

Fact	Inference		
○	○	**4. A.**	Burying trash takes up too much space.
○	○	**B.**	People now sort their trash.
○	○	**C.**	Many cities now help people recycle.
○	○	**D.**	Recycling saves space.

---

5. Each year during the last week in April, Mr. Mendez began his garden. He planted tomatoes during the second week in May. He weeded the garden as the plants grew. By the middle of summer, the tomatoes were ready to sell. Many people bought them. They liked his red, ripe tomatoes. By Labor Day it was time for Mr. Mendez to pull up all his tomato plants.

Fact	Inference		
○	○	**5. A.**	Mr. Mendez worked hard to grow tomatoes.
○	○	**B.**	The tomatoes were not good after Labor Day.
○	○	**C.**	He weeded the garden as the plants grew.
○	○	**D.**	He sold tomatoes for a very short time.

Lesson 3

1. Heavy trucks can destroy roads. To protect the roads, states make truck drivers weigh their cargo. They do this on giant scales at weigh stations along the road. The truck drives onto the scale, and its weight is taken. If the truck is too heavy, it is not allowed to drive any farther.

Fact	Inference		
○	○	**1. A.**	Heavy trucks can hurt roads.
○	○	**B.**	States make drivers weigh their cargo.
○	○	**C.**	Trucks must not be overloaded.
○	○	**D.**	Weigh stations have scales.

2. The gym was bright with colored lights. Crepe paper hung from the ceiling, and there was a band playing music. The music was so loud that people couldn't talk to one another. It was crowded in the gym, but no one was playing basketball or wearing gym clothes. All the girls were wearing dresses and flowers. All the boys were wearing suits.

Fact	Inference		
○	○	**2. A.**	There was a dance in the gym.
○	○	**B.**	The music was very loud.
○	○	**C.**	Basketball was not being played.
○	○	**D.**	Most people were dancing.

3. What can you do with trash and garbage? You can throw it away, or you can reuse some of it. A jar can be a vase for flowers or a place to store jewelry, money, or food. You can put fruit and vegetable scraps in the garden. You can also save newspapers. They can be made into clean paper.

Fact	Inference	
○	○	**3.** **A.** Some things can be used again.
○	○	**B.** New paper can be made from old.
○	○	**C.** A jar can be used in several ways.
○	○	**D.** Not all garbage needs to be thrown away.

---

4. Most people learn to sail on a small boat. While they are learning, they keep the boat in a protected spot, such as a harbor. First they learn the names of all the parts of the boat. Then they learn how to turn and move the boat with or against the wind. They also learn what to do if the boat turns over. Once people know how to sail a small boat, with practice they can sail a boat of almost any size.

Fact	Inference	
○	○	**4.** **A.** People best learn to sail on a small boat.
○	○	**B.** It is best to learn to sail in a protected spot.
○	○	**C.** Sailing takes some skill.
○	○	**D.** Large boats are harder to sail than small boats.

---

5. Schools need sprinklers. A sprinkler is like a shower. Sprinklers are installed in or near the ceilings. If a fire should start, the heat from the fire quickly melts a lead plug on the sprinkler. Once the plug melts, water rushes out of the showerlike heads. The water sprays out over a wide area.

Fact	Inference	
○	○	**5.** **A.** Sprinklers make schools safer.
○	○	**B.** Schools need sprinklers in case of fire.
○	○	**C.** Sprinklers have heads like showers.
○	○	**D.** Sprinklers can put out fires.

1. Airlines didn't have much money to build airports when they first flew planes between countries. Airlines designed airplanes that could land on the water. The bottom of the planes looked like boats. These planes could land anywhere there was water.

Fact   Inference

○   ○   **1. A.** It didn't cost much to land on water.

○   ○   **B.** Airplanes landed on water.

○   ○   **C.** Airlines didn't have much money to build airports.

○   ○   **D.** Very few planes land on water today.

---

2. Power lawn mowers make lawn care easy. Years ago people had to push a mower by hand. The push mower had three long blades that were attached to wheels on both sides. As the wheels turned, the blades spun and cut the grass. It took a long time to cut a lawn, especially when the grass was high. You had to be strong to push a mower like this. Today power lawn mowers come in all sizes. Some are so large that a person can ride on them.

Fact   Inference

○   ○   **2. A.** Power lawn mowers cut grass easily.

○   ○   **B.** It is hard to move a push mower.

○   ○   **C.** People ride on some mowers.

○   ○   **D.** Today mowers come in all sizes.

---

3. Mammals are animals that feed their young with milk. Pigs are the mammals that have the most babies. A pig can have as many as 34 babies at a time. A mother pig is called a sow. Baby pigs that are less than 10 weeks old are called piglets.

Fact   Inference

○   ○   **3. A.** Pigs feed their young with milk.

○   ○   **B.** Piglets are very small.

○   ○   **C.** Pigs are mammals.

○   ○   **D.** A pig can have up to 34 babies at a time.

4. The Pony Express carried letters from Missouri to California. Riders rode 10 miles and changed horses. They could put saddles on new horses in two minutes. Each rider had to change his horse seven times a day. The Pony Express was replaced by the telegraph. The telegraph sent messages over wires.

Fact	Inference		
○	○	**4. A.**	The Pony Express was slower than the telegraph.
○	○	**B.**	Riders changed horses after 10 miles.
○	○	**C.**	It was very tiring to be a Pony Express rider.
○	○	**D.**	Horses were worn out after 10 miles.

5. Parkside Hospital was holding a big bike race. Those who entered would help raise money for the hospital. Robin and Gwen decided to enter the 5-mile race. As the girls reached the end of the race, Gwen rode her bike over a hole in the road. She fell off and landed on the street. Although Robin was in the lead, she stopped to make sure Gwen was okay.

Fact	Inference		
○	○	**5. A.**	The race was 5 miles long.
○	○	**B.**	Robin and Gwen liked to ride bikes.
○	○	**C.**	Gwen fell off her bike.
○	○	**D.**	Robin was a helpful person.

1. Hummingbirds are the smallest birds. Some hummingbirds weigh less than a dime. They beat their wings very fast. Their wings beat up to 70 times a second. Because they are so active, they feed about once every 10 or 15 minutes. Hummingbirds are the only birds that can fly backwards.

Fact	Inference		
○	○	**1. A.**	Hummingbirds are very light.
○	○	**B.**	Hummingbirds can fly backwards.
○	○	**C.**	Hummingbirds beat their wings fast.
○	○	**D.**	Hummingbirds spend a lot of time eating.

2. Many books and movies have been written about the story of Robin Hood. Robin Hood was a folk hero who robbed the rich and gave what he took to the poor. Robin Hood is said to have lived in Sherwood Forest. He lived with a band of merry men. Many people have tried to prove he was a real person. So far no one has been able to show that he really lived.

Fact	Inference		
○	○	**2. A.**	Robin Hood is a popular story.
○	○	**B.**	People admire Robin Hood.
○	○	**C.**	Robin Hood cared about the poor.
○	○	**D.**	No one can prove that Robin Hood really lived.

3. Have you ever played with a yo-yo? Yo-yos were first used in the Philippines. They were not used as toys. Instead they were used for protection in the jungle. The word yo-yo means "to return" in the Philippine language. Today the yo-yo is a favorite toy in many countries.

Fact	Inference		
○	○	**3. A.**	Yo-yos are fun to play with.
○	○	**B.**	Yo-yos protected people from wild animals.
○	○	**C.**	Yo-yo means "to return."
○	○	**D.**	Today the yo-yo is a favorite toy.

4. In 1811, David Thompson was exploring the Rockies. He came across a large footprint. It was 14 inches long and 8 inches wide. The footprint was not the print of any known animal. Some people call the creature Bigfoot. More than 750 people say they have seen the hairy creature. It is said to be 8 feet tall and weigh 400 pounds.

Fact	Inference		
○	○	**4. A.**	Bigfoot may live in the Rockies.
○	○	**B.**	The footprint may have belonged to Bigfoot.
○	○	**C.**	More than 750 people say they have seen Bigfoot.
○	○	**D.**	Bigfoot may be 8 feet tall.

5. Hot dogs were named by a newspaper cartoonist from Chicago. One day in 1906, cartoonist Tad Dorgan was at a baseball game. A boy came by selling frankfurters. Dorgan drew a picture of the frankfurters. He made them look like small, long dogs on a bun. Under the cartoon he wrote, "Hot dogs."

Fact	Inference		
○	○	**5. A.**	Hot dogs were first called frankfurters.
○	○	**B.**	Tad Dorgan was a cartoonist.
○	○	**C.**	People liked the new name.
○	○	**D.**	Dorgan's cartoon was printed in the newspaper.

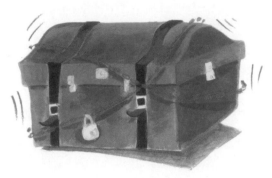

1. Harry Houdini was known
as "the escape king." He could escape
from iron boxes, straitjackets, and
even bank safes. Some of his most
exciting acts used water. People were often afraid that Houdini would not
escape, but he always got out safely. He was very strong, and he took good
care of his body.

Fact	Inference		
○	○	**1. A.**	Houdini took good care of his body.
○	○	**B.**	People were amazed by Houdini's escapes.
○	○	**C.**	Houdini could escape from a bank safe.
○	○	**D.**	People like to watch Houdini's acts.

2. The Taj Mahal is a beautiful building. It is made of snow-white marble.
It stands beside a river in Agra, India. The emperor of India had it built for
his wife. She died in 1630 at the age of 39. It took 20,000 men to build the
Taj Mahal. They worked for more than 22 years. The emperor had planned
for a building made of black marble across the river, but it was never built.

Fact	Inference		
○	○	**2. A.**	The Taj Mahal is in India.
○	○	**B.**	The Taj Mahal is made of white marble.
○	○	**C.**	The emperor wanted to honor his wife.
○	○	**D.**	The emperor loved his wife very much.

3. Marcie loved bananas. She loved banana splits, banana pudding, and
banana ice cream. Her favorite way to eat a banana was to simply peel it
and eat it. One day she had just enjoyed her favorite food while sitting on
the front steps of her house. She left the peel on the steps. An hour later her
mother came home. As she climbed the steps to the front door, she noticed
the peel. But it was too late.

Fact	Inference		
○	○	**3. A.**	Marcie left the peel on the steps.
○	○	**B.**	Marcie's mother slipped on the peel.
○	○	**C.**	Marcie loved bananas.
○	○	**D.**	Marcie's mother was angry.

4. Everyone knows what a tiger is, and everyone has heard of lions. Do you know what a "liger" is? A liger is a cross between a lion and a tiger. The first liger was born in the United States in 1948. It was born at the Hagh Zoo in Salt Lake City, Utah. If you had been there at the time, what would you have named it?

Fact	Inference	
◯	◯	**4. A.** A liger is a cross between a lion and a tiger.
◯	◯	**B.** Many people don't know about ligers.
◯	◯	**C.** Ligers were unusual animals in 1948.
◯	◯	**D.** Most ligers live in zoos.

5. Easter Island is in the South Pacific. More than 600 giant statues stand on the island. They are made of stone. Some are 70 feet tall. Some weigh up to 70 tons. For many years outsiders wondered how the statues were lifted into place. Then Thor Heyerdahl found the answer. He asked some island people to show him their methods. They raised a statue by pushing poles under its head. Thenthey pushed stones under it until it lifted into place.

Fact	Inference	
◯	◯	**5. A.** The statues were hard to raise upright.
◯	◯	**B.** Many statues stand on Easter Island.
◯	◯	**C.** Easter Island is in the South Pacific.
◯	◯	**D.** The people on Easter Island were quite clever.

1. Do you have to make your bed every day? Of course you don't really make the bed; you just straighten the sheets. The early Romans made beds by putting straw into cloth sacks. The straw then had to be removed every day to dry. People once really did make their beds every day, and that's where we got the saying.

Fact	Inference		
○	○	**1.** **A.**	The early Romans made beds of straw.
○	○	**B.**	The straw got damp during the night.
○	○	**C.**	Sleeping on damp beds was not comfortable.
○	○	**D.**	Today people don't sleep on straw beds.

2. P. T. Barnum loved to thrill crowds. He knew what would make them happy. No wonder he is known as the father of the modern circus. He started his "Greatest Show on Earth" in the 1870s. He had the huge elephant Jumbo and other strange creatures. He had clowns and singers, bearded ladies, and other odd acts. People flocked to his circus. Barnum's circus is still in business today.

Fact	Inference		
○	○	**2.** **A.**	Barnum started his circus in the 1870s.
○	○	**B.**	People liked Barnum's circus.
○	○	**C.**	Barnum was a smart businessperson.
○	○	**D.**	People enjoyed seeing bearded ladies.

3. Cows are grass-eating animals. Grass is not easy to chew. Because of this, cows have a special way of making sure they chew it well. They chew a little grass and then swallow it. Then the grass makes its way from the cow's stomach back to its mouth. The cow then chews the grass again. This is called chewing cud.

Fact	Inference		
○	○	**3. A.**	Grass is difficult to chew.
○	○	**B.**	A cow's stomach helps it chew the grass well.
○	○	**C.**	Chewing grass over again is called chewing cud.
○	○	**D.**	Grass is an important food for cows.

---

4. Most people don't like to do chores around the house. Scientists studied this topic. They found that most people don't like washing dishes. They also do not enjoy cleaning the bathroom.

Fact	Inference		
○	○	**4. A.**	Scientists asked people about chores.
○	○	**B.**	Most people don't like washing dishes.
○	○	**C.**	They would rather use a dishwasher.
○	○	**D.**	Most people don't like household chores.

---

5. Dogs are sometimes called "man's best friend," but some dogs are friendlier than others. Some dogs bite many more people than others do. The kind of dog that bites the most is the German police dog. Poodles also often bite people. Sheepdogs, on the other hand, do not bite much at all.

Fact	Inference		
○	○	**5. A.**	German police dogs are not good pets.
○	○	**B.**	Poodles often bite people.
○	○	**C.**	Sheepdogs are friendly.
○	○	**D.**	Dogs are called "man's best friend."

1. Have you ever seen a bullfight? A person stands in a large ring and waves a red cape at a bull. Then the bull runs at the cape, and the person scampers out of the way. You might think that the red color of the cape makes the bull angry, but this is not true. In fact the bull is color-blind, so it cannot tell red from other colors. The bull charges at the motion of the cape, not the color of it.

Fact	Inference	
○	○	**1.** **A.** In a bullfight a person stands in a ring.
○	○	**B.** Red capes are used in bullfights.
○	○	**C.** Bulls are color-blind.
○	○	**D.** A bull would charge a green cape.

2. Imagine that you are sitting in a wheelchair. You need to get to the third floor of a building. First, you need to avoid the steps in front, so you look for a ramp. To open the heavy door, you look for a button to push. Once inside, you need to avoid the stairway, so you look for an elevator. No problem! Most buildings built today have a special design so that wheelchair users can move around safely.

Fact	Inference	
○	○	**2.** **A.** Wheelchair users go up ramps and elevators.
○	○	**B.** Most older buildings did not have a special design.
○	○	**C.** Wheelchair users need to avoid steps.
○	○	**D.** Many new buildings have a special design.

3. Cheryl had never tried to fix her bicycle before. But her bike had a flat tire, and it needed to be fixed. No one else had offered to help, so Cheryl decided to try to fix the flat tire herself.

Fact	Inference	
○	○	**3.** **A.** Cheryl wasn't sure she could fix her bike.
○	○	**B.** The bike had a flat tire.
○	○	**C.** Cheryl wanted to ride her bike.
○	○	**D.** No one else offered to help.

4. Cleopatra lived more than 2,000 years ago. At the age of 18, she became the queen of Egypt. She ruled with her brothers, but both of them died. Cleopatra then became the only ruler of her land. She was not a great queen. She taxed her people heavily. She held control of the throne until her death at the age of 39.

Fact	Inference	
○	○	**4. A.** Cleopatra first ruled with her brothers.
○	○	**B.** She was the queen of Egypt.
○	○	**C.** The people of Egypt did not like Cleopatra.
○	○	**D.** Cleopatra died at age 39.

5. The smell of liver made Wally hold his nose, and he thought he would be sick each time he had to taste spinach. Yet there before him sat those two foods, just waiting to be eaten. When his mother left the room, Wally dashed to the window. He scraped his plate clean behind the curtains and hurried back to his seat. When his mother returned, she was surprised at how quickly he had finished his meal. Wally only grinned nervously.

Fact	Inference	
○	○	**5. A.** Wally doesn't like liver or spinach.
○	○	**B.** Wally's mother was surprised he had finished.
○	○	**C.** Wally scraped his plate behind the curtains.
○	○	**D.** Wally was supposed to eat liver and spinach.

Writing Roundup

Read each story. Then read the question that follows it. Write your answers on the lines below each question.

1. A huge wave blasted onto the deck. The few pieces of equipment that hadn't been tied down were washed away. The whistle for help sounded just before another monster of a wave slammed down. This one shattered a fire hose box, and the hose in the box fell and then moved across the deck like a snake.

What is happening?

_____

_____

_____

2. Devin always thought the game looked easy. Now she had a different idea. The ball was very heavy. She found it hard to knock down the pins at the end of the alley.

What game is Devin learning?

_____

_____

_____

3. The captain called out Javier's name. Javier marched to the front of the line. He proudly gave a salute.

What is Javier?

_____

_____

_____

Read the paragraph below. Then answer the questions.

Teresa never misses a workout. Unlike most of the students who use the high school's training gym, Teresa stays away from the weights. She rides the bicycles and runs on the treadmill. She also jumps rope a lot of the time. Teresa does all this with a plan in mind. She expects to run in a marathon race in the future. She wants to stay thin and able to run long distances. Teresa has a fine plan for now, but she still needs a coach's help. She needs someone to give her special facts about training for a marathon.

1. Why doesn't Teresa use weights?

_____

_____

2. Why does Teresa try to stay thin?

_____

_____

3. What kind of person is Teresa?

_____

_____

4. How could a coach help Teresa?

_____

_____

Check Yourself

Unit 1

What Are Facts?

p. 6

Fact: The *Titanic* ran into an iceberg and sank.

Fact: The ship ran into the iceberg on April 14, 1912.

Practice Finding Facts

p. 7

3. A

Lesson 1
pp. 8–9
1. C   6. C
2. A   7. D
3. B   8. A
4. D   9. C
5. A   10. D

Lesson 2
pp. 10–11
1. B   6. C
2. A   7. A
3. C   8. B
4. B   9. C
5. C   10. D

Lesson 3
pp. 12–13
1. B   6. B
2. A   7. C
3. C   8. B
4. A   9. A
5. D   10. A

Lesson 4
pp. 14–15
1. B   6. B
2. C   7. C
3. D   8. C
4. B   9. D
5. D   10. A

Lesson 5
pp. 16–17
1. B   6. C
2. A   7. B
3. C   8. D
4. C   9. C
5. D   10. A

Lesson 6
pp. 18–19
1. B   6. D
2. C   7. A
3. D   8. D
4. D   9. A
5. C   10. C

Lesson 7
pp. 20–21
1. B   6. A
2. C   7. C
3. B   8. B
4. A   9. D
5. D   10. C

Lesson 8
pp. 22–23
1. B   6. C
2. C   7. D
3. B   8. B
4. A   9. B
5. D   10. C

Writing Roundup

p. 24

Possible answers include:

1. The earl of Sandwich invented the sandwich.

2. The sandwich was invented in the 1700s.

3. The first sandwich was made of two slices of bread with roast meat in between.

p. 25
Check that you have four facts in your paragraph.

Unit 2

What Is Sequence?

p. 26
2, 1, 3

Practice with Sequence

p. 27
3. C

Lesson 1
pp. 28–29
1. 2, 1, 3
2. B
3. A
4. B
5. B

Lesson 2
pp. 30–31
1. 1, 3, 2
2. B
3. B
4. C
5. B

Lesson 3
pp. 32–33
1. 3, 1, 2
2. A
3. A
4. B
5. A

Lesson 4
pp. 34–35
1. 3, 1, 2
2. B
3. B
4. B
5. C

Lesson 5
pp. 36–37
1. 3, 2, 1
2. B
3. A
4. C
5. A

Lesson 6
pp. 38–39
1. 2, 1, 3
2. C
3. A
4. B
5. A

Lesson 7
pp. 40–41
1. 1, 3, 2
2. B
3. A
4. C
5. B

Lesson 8
pp. 42–43
1. 3, 2, 1
2. B
3. A
4. C
5. B

Writing Roundup

p. 44

Possible answers include:

1. First, two sets of doors close and lock.

2. A set of weights goes down while cables pull the car up.

3. When the car reaches the chosen floor, brakes hold the car in place.

4. The doors open, and people get out.

p. 45

Check that your story is written in sequence.

Check that you have used time order words, such as first, next, and last.

Unit 3

Working with Context

p. 47

2. A
3. B

LESSON 1 · pp. 48–49

1. C	9. A
2. B	10. B
3. D	11. B
4. C	12. A
5. A	13. D
6. C	14. B
7. A	15. B
8. D	16. A

LESSON 2 · pp. 50–51

1. B	9. A
2. D	10. B
3. B	11. B
4. C	12. D
5. C	13. B
6. D	14. C
7. C	15. B
8. C	16. A

LESSON 3 · pp. 52–53

1. C	9. B
2. D	10. C
3. D	11. D
4. B	12. B
5. C	13. B
6. B	14. A
7. B	15. C
8. C	16. B

LESSON 4 · pp. 54–55

1. A	9. D
2. D	10. C
3. B	11. A
4. D	12. C
5. A	13. C
6. C	14. A
7. A	15. B
8. C	16. D

LESSON 5 · pp. 56–57

1. B	5. B
2. C	6. B
3. B	7. A
4. B	8. A

LESSON 6 · pp. 58–59

1. D	5. C
2. B	6. B
3. A	7. A
4. C	8. D

LESSON 7 · pp. 60–61

1. C	5. D
2. B	6. B
3. D	7. A
4. B	8. B

LESSON 8 · pp. 62–63

1. B	5. A
2. C	6. B
3. D	7. C
4. C	8. C

Writing Roundup

p. 64

Possible answers include:

1. umbrella or raincoat
2. head or clothes
3. drum or tuba
4. play or march
5. nails or wood
6. strange or wonderful

p. 65

Possible answers include

1. She dug deeper.
   She ran for help.

2. It was a bag of coins.
   It was a ring she had lost.

3. She would look for the owner.
   She would put it in a safe place.

4. She could walk dogs. She could
   be a pet sitter.

5. She was going on vacation.
   She needed help with her yard.

6. She will water Ms. Fielder's
   plants. She will mow Ms.
   Fielder's yard.

Unit 4

**Practice Finding
the Main Idea**

p. 67

2. The correct answer is D. The
paragraph is about the lives of lion
cubs. The number of cubs that are
born is a detail. The paragraph
doesn't really tell how hyenas
and leopards hunt. We can tell
that they hunt lion cubs because
the mother lion wants to keep
her cubs safe from them. The
paragraph does not tell anything
about the weight of cubs at birth.

LESSON 1 · pp. 68–69

1. C
2. A
3. A
4. B
5. B

LESSON 2 · pp. 70–71

1. A
2. B
3. C
4. B
5. A

LESSON 3 · pp. 72–73

1. D
2. C
3. D
4. C
5. A

LESSON 4 · pp. 74–75

1. A
2. B
3. A
4. D
5. B

LESSON 5 · pp. 76–77

1. B
2. A
3. C
4. B
5. A

LESSON 6 · pp. 78–79

1. D
2. C
3. A
4. A
5. D

LESSON 7 · pp. 80–81

1. A
2. A
3. A
4. C
5. D

LESSON 8 · pp. 82–83

1. C
2. C
3. D
4. C
5. B

Writing Roundup

p. 84

Possible answers include:

1. A few rabbits were set free
   and caused a big problem
   in Australia.

2. Tom Bradley was an African
   American man who did a lot
   for Los Angeles.

3. A Native American actor
   became famous because of
   a tear.

p. 85

Check that you have
underlined your main idea.

Check that you have used
four details in your story.

Unit 5

Using What You Know

p. 87

Fall or autumn, Thanksgiving,
Fourth of July, Valentine's Day

Lesson 1
pp. 88–89
1. C
2. A
3. A
4. B
5. C

Lesson 2
pp. 90–91
1. B
2. C
3. A
4. C
5. D

Lesson 3
pp. 92–93
1. B
2. B
3. C
4. A
5. D

Lesson 4
pp. 94–95
1. C
2. C
3. A
4. B
5. B

Lesson 5
pp. 96–97
1. C
2. B
3. B
4. A
5. A

Lesson 6
pp. 98–99
1. B
2. B
3. B
4. D
5. D

Lesson 7
pp. 100–101
1. D
2. B
3. D
4. D
5. C

Lesson 8
pp. 102–103
1. D
2. D
3. C
4. C
5. D

Writing Roundup

p. 104

Possible answers include:

1. Jim Thorpe could play many sports.

2. Ms. is the newest title of respect for a woman.

3. Oprah Winfrey did not start out as a star.

p. 105

Possible answers include:

1. Paco's grandfather doesn't live with Paco. He is sharing Paco's room while visiting.

2. Paco and his grandfather probably don't have the same last name. This grandfather is the father of Paco's mother.

3. Texas became a state in 1845. Paco's family moved to Texas in 1847, two years after Texas became a state.

4. Paco's grandfather isn't interested in finding more family in Mexico. He says it seems as if they've always been in Texas.

Unit 6

Practice Making Inferences

p. 107
2. A. F   B. I   C. I   D. F

Lesson 1
pp. 108–109
1. A. I   B. I   C. F   D. F
2. A. I   B. I   C. F   D. F
3. A. F   B. F   C. I   D. I
4. A. I   B. F   C. I   D. I
5. A. F   B. F   C. I   D. I

Lesson 2
pp. 110–111
1. A. F   B. F   C. I   D. I
2. A. I   B. F   C. I   D. F
3. A. I   B. F   C. F   D. I
4. A. F   B. I   C. F   D. I
5. A. I   B. I   C. F   D. I

Lesson 3
pp. 112–113
1. A. F   B. F   C. I   D. F
2. A. I   B. I   C. F   D. I
3. A. F   B. F   C. F   D. I
4. A. I   B. I   C. I   D. I
5. A. I   B. I   C. F   D. I

Lesson 4
pp. 114–115
1. A. I   B. F   C. F   D. I
2. A. I   B. I   C. F   D. F
3. A. I   B. F   C. F   D. F
4. A. I   B. F   C. I   D. I
5. A. F   B. I   C. F   D. I

Lesson 5
pp. 116–117
1. A. I   B. F   C. F   D. I
2. A. I   B. I   C. I   D. F
3. A. I   B. I   C. F   D. F
4. A. I   B. I   C. F   D. F
5. A. I   B. F   C. I   D. I

Lesson 6
pp. 118–119
1. A. F   B. I   C. F   D. I
2. A. F   B. F   C. I   D. I
3. A. F   B. I   C. F   D. I
4. A. F   B. I   C. I   D. I
5. A. I   B. F   C. F   D. I

Lesson 7
pp. 120–121
1. A. F   B. I   C. I   D. I
2. A. F   B. I   C. I   D. I
3. A. F   B. I   C. F   D. I
4. A. I   B. F   C. I   D. F
5. A. I   B. F   C. I   D. F

Lesson 8
pp. 122–123
1. A. F   B. F   C. F   D. I
2. A. F   B. I   C. F   D. F
3. A. I   B. F   C. I   D. I
4. A. F   B. I   C. I   D. F
5. A. I   B. F   C. F   D. I

Writing Roundup

p. 124

Possible answers include:

1. A ship is being hit by a storm.

2. Devin is learning to bowl.

3. Javier is a soldier.

p. 125

Possible answers include:

4. Teresa doesn't think weights help with marathon running.

5. Teresa thinks marathon runners need to be thin.

6. Teresa is dependable, hardworking, and serious.

7. A coach could tell Teresa what she may not know about training for a marathon.